W9-AON-873

THE WASTE LAND

AND

OTHER WRITINGS

T. S. ELIOT

THE
WASTE LAND
AND
OTHER WRITINGS

Introduction by Mary Karr

THE MODERN LIBRARY

NEW YORK

2001 Modern Library Edition

Biographical note copyright © 2001 by Random House, Inc.
Introduction copyright © 2001 by Mary Karr

LIBRARY OF CONGRESS CATALOGING-IN-PUBLICATION DATA
Eliot, T. S. (Thomas Stearns), 1888–1965.
The waste land and other writings/T. S. Eliot;
introduction by Mary Karr.
p.   cm.
ISBN 0-679-64101-7 (alk. paper)
I. Title
PS3509.L43 A6   2001
821'.912—dc21   00-64571

Modern Library website address: www.modernlibrary.com

Printed in the United States of America on acid-free paper

2 4 6 8 9 7 5 3

T. S. ELIOT

Thomas Stearns Eliot was born in St. Louis, Missouri, on September 26, 1888. He was educated at Harvard, and then at Merton College, Oxford; after attending the latter he decided to remain in England. He worked as a teacher, then at a bank, and then as an editor at the publishing house of Faber and Gwyer (later Faber & Faber), which he joined in 1925.

Eliot's first major poem, "The Love Song of J. Alfred Prufrock," appeared in the magazine *Poetry* in 1915. Its publication was facilitated by Ezra Pound; the literary friendship between the two would remain an important influence on Eliot. "The Waste Land" was published in 1922; it led to worldwide recognition. In 1922 Eliot also founded the magazine *Criterion*. His criticism, published there and elsewhere, was as influential as his verse.

In 1927 Eliot joined the Church of England. He continued to publish important works, notably "Ash Wednesday" (1930); the plays *Murder in the Cathedral* (1935) and *The Family Reunion* (1939); *Old Possum's Book of Practical Cats* (1939); *Four Quartets* (1943), the critical work *Notes Toward the Definition of Culture* (1948); and the play *The Cocktail Party* (1949).

Eliot was awarded the Nobel Prize for literature in 1948. He died on January 4, 1965, in London.

Contents

HOW TO READ "THE WASTE LAND" SO IT ALTERS YOUR SOUL RATHER THAN JUST ADDLING YOUR HEAD

Mary Karr

The boundary between twentieth-century verse in English and its nineteenth-century predecessors—Romantic poetry and the genteel Victorian stuff after it—didn't simply dissolve. It came down with an axe swoop, and the blade was T. S. Eliot's "Waste Land." William Carlos Williams said the poem "wiped out our world as if an atom bomb had been dropped upon it." Its publication in 1922 killed off the last limping, rickets-ridden vestiges of the old era and raised the flag of Modernism, under whose flapping shadow we still live.

By this, I mean that the poem exists as a kind of seminal instant for the aesthetic (and, in some circles, moral) values we espouse. The techniques it teaches are reference and irony, self-mockery and obliquity. These are the same ones championed today in art and culture at all levels—be it David Letterman's hipper-than-thou sarcasm or the erotic self-mockery of Cindy Sherman's photographs. Quentin Tarantino's nonlinear jumps between scenes in *Pulp Fiction* partly derive from it; as does the oracular, disaffected voice of Cormac McCarthy in *Blood Meridian* or the dreamy surface of Toni Morrison's *Beloved.*

It's also the gold standard for difficulty in modern poetry, the measured point on the this-is-hard chart literary specialists still tend to laser-point to. A recent issue of the literary mag *Parnassus* held no fewer than four references to Eliot—his titanic status and religiosity, and how infamously murky "Waste Land" is while being "encrusted with learning." I've been as guilty as any critic or academic of invoking the poem in essays and lectures as a voodoo mojo to vanquish the lesser spirits of my own intellectual insecurity.

It can have similarly totemic powers for creative writers, who tend to wave its name as a kind of passport into the infernal regions of artistic obscurity. It's the historical document that permits a young poet to say, *Well, my work isn't nearly this impenetrable, so stop telling me to rewrite for clarity when you're just being small-minded and lazy.* Perhaps Randall Jarrell first used its difficulty in this way, to indict his era's readers (or nonreaders) back in 1951:

> When a person says accusingly that he can't understand Eliot, his tone implies that most of his happiest hours are spent at the fireside among worn copies of the *Agamemnon, Phedre,* and the Symbolic Works of William Blake....

A frustrated reader can also gesture to the poem's impenetrability to justify why he or she avoids poetry at all, saying, *If this is poetry, then I'm heading for the nearest channel changer.*

So for good or ill, the poem is one of the literary instants we're still either evolving or devolving from (depending on your viewpoint) as a people.

Yet people don't read it anymore. Whole flocks of college students who've come under my tutelage at Syracuse University recently profess to not having *heard* of it—along with much else written before Elvis. A search on the web under "The Waste Land" hooks you up with a TV show.

That said: Not to read it is to pretend that we of this twenty-first century have drawn ourselves whole (M. C. Escher–like) from our own heads. It's to ignore history, taking on faith that what now seems beautiful or important or right in terms of reading or listening or watching has no source other than this time, this place.

Isn't that equally true, you might say, of Homer or Milton? Of course, but I don't see students trying to pass off twenty-line Homeric similes digressing from epic battle narratives as experimental form. Which is precisely what happens with Eliot.

For "The Waste Land"'s techniques continue to define what we think of as avant-garde even among those who eschew actually reading Eliot because he's a dead white guy who represents the *old* guard.

This spring, for instance, I found myself explaining to a young writer that the creative prose he'd turned in shifted voices and scenes in a dislocating way—a kind way of saying it made no sense. I was then painstakingly told that this was part of an edgy new trend in fiction—nonlinear narrative that uses shifting multiple voices peppered with hermetic references. So he was, he went on, *intentionally* doling out the names of TV shows I hadn't watched and bands I hadn't heard. If you substitute his references to *Brady Bunch* reruns for Eliot's Dante, you're in "Waste Land"–ville. This student was smart and a great reader who had been penned into a theory-based curriculum that kept him from much actual literature. Once I recounted the long tradition of his allegedly radical method, he blanched and went on to the hard work of rewriting that students often balk at. (His bravura approach is not unusual: at his age I also subscribed to that formula made popular by its breathtaking ease: *first word = best word*.)

Let's say you're one of the few who has read "The Waste Land": Why reread it? Once you've absorbed its historical consequences, why not leave it back there with dusty documents like the Declaration of Independence?

Because it's beautiful, though intricate and spiritually desolate in the angst and squalor it sails me through. I read it to hear a noise that tells me about certain states of mind so horrible I live much of my life trying to deny their existence though they swarm at the periphery of my eyes during late-night startles. These states are indescribable if you live through them and all but unknowable if you don't, except, perhaps, through the aegis of this particular poem.

Read incorrectly, "The Waste Land" makes the average reader feel dumb. That was true upon its publication seventy-eight years ago and remains so. By "incorrectly," I don't mean to red-pencil an X across anybody's approach to poetry in general or to these pages specifically. Just the opposite. In this country, literature from the past mostly gets taught to aggravate a reader's insecurity.

In fact, any potential reader should banish all nay-saying voices, or at least crank down the volume on them. Then amble good-naturedly up to these allegedly daunting pages with simian curiosity. Presume there's something gorgeous and life altering about this poem, then set out to find it. In fact, 95 percent of its splendor exists on the surface and can be gleaned minus a comparative literature degree. Yet fear of looking dumb often springboards readers from that surface— either into some scholarly chasm of reference work and scholarship from which they never return or into the void of not reading at all.

In terms of shape, the poem is a collage, somewhat disparate pieces assembled to create in readers the kind of despair that infected much of Western Europe after the Great War. England and America (among other countries) had fed hordes of its young men into that conflict, which wasn't unusual for a war. But the First World War also delivered the blindest, most efficient machine for carnage to date. Sure the Chinese had passed gunpowder along to Marco Polo, and there'd been the remoteness of catapults and cannon fire for centuries, but the First War's air battles and chemical weaponry broadened the bloodbath's scope. Airplanes could fly over and dismantle troops where they stood. Mustard gas could creep across the fields into trenches to scorch lung tissue and other soft membranes. Such slaughter could also now be captured effectively on film and shipped home. (The first box camera from George Eastman in 1888 had seen myriad improvements by 1914.) Wireless communication also made accurate reportage of distant campaigns transmittable.

With that war, the glory of dying for one's country as expressed by Horace in the line *"Dulce et decorum est pro patria mori"* became a darkly ironic notion when Wilfred Owen used the Latin sentence as the title for a seminal antiwar poem shortly before being killed in action. By World War II, Eliot's poetic influence was being felt in poems that were exponentially more bitter and graphic. It's Eliot who permits Jarrell to step over Horace's mournful sense of honor by rawly rendering the Second World War's grotesqueries. The last line of Jarrell's "The Death of the Ball Turret Gunner" reads: "When I died they washed me out of the turret with a hose."

This wholesale motorized murder was part and parcel of the increasingly mechanized world that had been assembling since the first cotton gins and mills marked the Industrial Revolution. The notion of technological progress heaped lifestyle changes on the Western world more radical, perhaps, than written history ever recorded. Lightbulbs banished night, and instruments of velocity like steamships and airplanes were shrinking the Earth's distances. The first subways opened in London in 1890 to whisk human beings through underground chasms in herds. As cars began to replace buggies, cities ceased to be designed around human traffic and began to be built to accommodate vehicles, often eradicating pedestrian traffic in the process. Buildings ceased to approach human scale and scraped the heavens. You need only compare modern-day Los Angeles with Paris to grasp how those looming, boxlike structures combined with newfound bustle and clanking whatnots to isolate and estrange various urban citizenries.

So expect a text fragmented as a clattering, bouncy ride through London or New York must've been; a text disorienting as modern battle was to the soldiers of the Great War. The poem's made of bits and overlays, snatches of speech and songs—various dictions and noises and tones. Just as cities were.

Much of poetry's game in the past two centuries has been seeing what a writer can shoehorn into verse. Prior to the nineteenth century, subject and character, form and even diction were sorely conscribed—what you could write about and how. Eliot's partly responsible for opening those gates. "The Waste Land" gets a lot in. You'll hit a sibyl pronouncing in Greek her longing to die. There's an Australian drinking song. Dante's language is there, and so is chitchat overheard in a pub. There's Homer's blind seer Tiresias, the "old man with wrinkled dugs" and a wacky clairvoyant with a bogus tarot pack.

This collage technique of Eliot's is now amply used in all manner of media—whether plastic or performance arts, or in other texts.

In contemporary movies and novels, characters and story lines may remain entirely disconnected as in "The Waste Land." The critically acclaimed film *Magnolia* (1999) featured about a dozen paths that never crossed save for a gratuitous underlying link with the same game show. That work, like Eliot's, also blends high culture with low, the simpleminded with the transcendent.

But "The Waste Land" jacks up the difficulty quotient even higher in three specific ways. 1) The author's notes, written in a somewhat dodgy and sometimes coy tone, tend to confuse rather than illuminate the poem's references, its quotes and quirks. 2) The untranslated languages make sense only to a polyglot. 3) Add to those difficulties the fact that Eliot borrowed heavily from the poetic techniques of the French Symbolists, whose poems sported mysterious surfaces and private symbologies rather than inherited myths and the familiar rhetorical poses that were part of agreed-upon cultural norms.

The author's notes drew critical interest from the get-go and went on to generate the antlike industry of Ph.D. candidates for generations. Perhaps some foresight of Eliot's about the ascendancy of academic criticism caused him to drop these notes as bread crumbs to entice or intimidate critics. Peter Ackroyd's biography of Eliot claims that the first reviews in England were "variously baffled and respectful"—partly because of the notes and references, which left some critics mystified enough that they *couldn't* come out and say they didn't like the poem for fear their ignorance of his learned and sophisticated methods would be discovered. (Poets and prosers alike have been packaging incomprehensibility as brilliant experiment ever since.)

It's a little-recognized fact that the controversial notes were an afterthought Eliot later considered cutting because they so distracted readers from the poem. In fact, he'd only tacked them on because the nineteen-page poem alone didn't seem long enough to constitute a book. One letter suggests that he also considered fluffing out the book with Ezra Pound's masterful edits, or, alternately, of publishing the sections as separate poems in the *Dial* and the *Criterion*—an idea Pound also disabused him of.

Even knowing the randomness of the notes' insertion, you still can't ignore them wholesale. There they squat in the text. But once you stop cowing in their shadow, you can decipher them as whimsical rather than smug. Read that way, the notes change tone, and the gates of the poem may start to widen. Till then, they can leave a timid reader feeling both bone-headed and teased—facing a string of intentionally vague *nyah nyah's* at what you don't know. The notes are capricious and shifting in both purpose and attitude.

For one thing, there just isn't much constancy to what gets a note and what doesn't. Often (but not always) it's a reference in another tongue. The first German snippet you hit (line twelve) doesn't warrant a source, maybe because it's conversation and not from a specific text. Then twenty lines later, you stumble on a four-line swatch of Wagner libretto. The endnote for that reads "*V. Tristan und Isolde,* I, verses 5–8." Which tells contemporary readers—including those who don't know Wagner and those who do—virtually nothing.

Grad students trained to track down the sources tend to bound after the origin of such references with the automatic energy of dogs loping after any thrown Frisbee. But such trackings down don't yield much relative to the poem. Even listening to the Wagner, the note and reference don't bring much to the proverbial interpretive party. Some argue that the notes contribute absolutely nil.

The fact that he's always guessing stuff just augments the breezy tone. He doesn't know where one drinking song comes from; can't remember which Antarctic expedition "stimulated" some writing—"I think one of Shackleton's. . . ." Or here's Eliot's wiseassed note on an early scene: "I am not familiar with the exact constitution of the Tarot pack of cards, from which I have obviously departed to suit my own convenience." Today, I interpret Eliot's pose here not as pompous but as a self-mocking signal, a bold admission that the notes *are* trivial. I also wonder whether plagiarism laws of his age required such notations. Or Eliot's manner may be construed as scorn for that requirement or of the academy's notions of "truth" in general.

Ultimately, the references have an almost sentimental feel, and I've come to treat them that way. The reference to Wagner, for instance, sits like some souvenir paperweight from a Swiss mountain holiday, the type you might find on display in a Victorian interior. The object's aesthetic virtues are wholly private, its evocative value zilch except to whoever bought it. Nothing in its corporeal form—let's say it's a bronze bear—conjures the experience of snow and sun it alludes to. I tend to picture Eliot's childhood parlor as a many-tabled room replete with such objects. Taking tea in such a place, you'd allot no time to such objects. So if the notes are dogging you, think of them that way, then try according them the same measure of attention.

But why use foreign languages and high-brow references in the first place? During Eliot's day, the intelligentsia thought of itself as keeper of some cultural flame that was threatening to snuff out. They were partly right. Only 4 percent of the populace in Eliot's day went to college, compared to about 40 percent in 1980.

Eliot was born in 1888, when bombastic Victorian poems were flooding magazines in English alongside the self-conscious, long-winded twaddle of poets like Swinburne, who fancied themselves decadent, sometimes even submitting poems on mauve paper. Tennyson had been the last great poet in English, mastering the sweeping albeit empty rhetorical gesture that "The Waste Land" stands in opposition to: "Tears, idle tears, I know not what they mean, . . ." Tennyson's lengthy *In Memoriam* includes (among other things) convoluted arguments about how the existence of God isn't provable by the universe's design—an ideology commonly used then to reconcile faith with reason. The poem ultimately says it's how you *feel* that proves God's presence. In other words, the poem can be summarized fairly easily in prose. That poetry would be generated in service of such a prosaic enterprise seems ludicrous today.

But that's mostly what poetry was doing in those days—batting cleanup for prose and sermons. While novelists like Conrad and Hardy and James were cranking out novels that represented aspects of contemporary life in a fresh way, poets were fancifying old sermon topics with a kind of Matthew Arnold solemnity. Even Edwin Arlington Robinson, whose poems of the 1920s are psychologically resonant and darkly ironic in a modern way ("Richard Cory," "Mr. Flood's Party"), wrote three endlessly long, irrelevant poems on the legend of King Arthur.

Walt Whitman's song from the nineteenth century was also reverberating across the country in this ghastly faux-rustic form. "Lyrical effortless effusion" was high praise. Poetry was written for ship launches and fair openings, the cutting of library ribbons. Harvard critic David Perkins says, "The 1890s seemed to have happened for the sole purpose of having Eliot decimate them." His two-volume history of Modern poetry drums up some of the best examples of what Eliot was trying to counter. There were schools of handyman poets, including one guy whose wife submitted his poems to *Scribner's* (then a popular magazine). Her note reads: "My husband has always been a successful blacksmith. Now he's old and his mind is slowly weakening, so he has taken to writing poems, several of which I enclose herewith." Read *Backlog Ballads* or *Pensive Pansies,* and you'll perhaps find yourself thirsting for Eliot's quotes from Homer and Dante. I doubt he'd have the same agenda today. But imagine writing in a time when armies of poets seemed intent on ignoring poetry's rich history from other cultures and languages in order to scribble the kind of automatic blather that filled popular magazines. Maybe then you'll comprehend Eliot's peppering of the poem with ancient references. I try to comprehend Eliot's need to put the notes in without being tyrannized by them.

"The Waste Land" also shows Eliot's formal innovations, for he draws a level bead on that clopping and long-beaten iambic horse that trotted through most Victorian and Pre-Raphaelite stuff. Many of those poets seemed to have written solely by filling in metered pigeonholes with what Ezra Pound called "vacuums and slush."

After Eliot left Harvard, he moved to England and fell under the spell of Pound, who was perhaps even more lingo crazed than his equally provincial but somewhat neurasthenic charge. Pound also shared Eliot's commitment to save the culture from boneheads. His *Cantos* contain twenty-one languages (including five dead ones), and in *ABC of Reading* he recommends (a mild word for what he does) that any poet worth her salt should master Old French to read Arnaut Daniel, enough Latin to plow through Catullus, enough Greek for Homer and Sappho.

In those years, Pound was prancing around London disguised as an American aborigine, wearing a cape and pointy mustache, challenging people to duels and so forth, but he savored Eliot's music as perhaps no one had before. And his method for reading certainly mirrored "The Waste Land"'s:

> The way to study Shakespeare's language is to study it side by side with something different and of equal extent. The proper antagonist is Dante, who is of equal size and DIFFERENT. To study Shakespeare's language merely in comparison with the DECADENCE of the same thing doesn't give one's mind any leverage.

Pound would later write, "Relations between things are more important than the things themselves." Or, as some soul singer says, "It ain't the meat; it's the motion."

Which might well have been the French Symbolist manifesto, if those poets hadn't so loathed ideology as to scorn manifestos. They were so iconoclastic that talking about them as a school at all is somewhat contrived. Still, it's fair enough to say that some French poets between about 1860 and 1885—Baudelaire, Mallarmé, Rimbaud, Laforgue, Valéry—seemed to have evolved the slippery modus operandi Eliot made use of in "The Waste Land." Critic Arthur Symons wrote of Symbolism:

> It is all an attempt to spiritualize literature, to evade the old bondage of rhetoric . . . of exteriority. Description is banished that beautiful things might be evoked, magically: the regular beat of verse is broken that words may fly, upon subtler wings. Mystery is no longer feared, as the great mystery in whose midst we are islanded was feared by those to whom that unknown sea was only a great void.

The Symbolists summoned poems from the ethereal. Scholarly or didactic readers desperately seeking "meaning" in such poems may impatiently wave away all the sea mist and opium haze, thus missing the heady aromas intended as the central poetic experience.

Again, seen in the context of history, such smoke-and-mirrors methods make exquisite sense. Late-nineteenth-century poets in English seemed to be writing almost devoid of musical or aesthetic concerns, both of which were so central to Symbolism. It was more common to reflect moral ideals of the most philistine nature—a soldier's honor, a mother's love, the virtue of hard work, etc.—in standardized packages.

Take up a card with a kitten on it at your local drugstore, and you'll know what I mean here. The terms of such poems are presumed to be agreed upon by the culture at large, so that from the first line you can easily predict the last and most moves in between. Sentimentalism is simply emotion that hasn't been argued for or proven to a reader, only gestured to. Such hackneyed moves signal the writer's disinterest in his subject and usually prompt the reader's eyes to lose focus. You know that soporific instant in a poem or novel when your head starts saying *blah blah blah* and your eyes start swiftly swimming to the page bottom? Any announcement to the reader of the generalized or automatic warrants such detachment from the text. If you encounter a concrete poem typographically shaped like a hammer using the words *bam bam bam bam,* you just won't bother to *read* every single bam. Nor should you.

Eliot meant above all to keep the reader riveted to the text and concentratedly alive. So each word might have heft, so the reader wouldn't be lulled or dulled into glazing over words once the poem's argument was absorbed. A constantly shifting surface without argued transitions forces you into alertness if you're to keep up with the poem's changing terms.

So most of "The Waste Land" "means" only by ricochet, never in direct statement. Meaning in the typical sense wasn't something he was chasing. It was only used:

> . . . to satisfy one habit of the reader, to keep his mind diverted and quiet, while the poem does its work upon him: much as the

imaginary burglar is always provided with a bit of nice meat for the house-dog.

Instead, "The Waste Land"'s meaning is inexorably entwined with the music, the variety of noises and how they jam together, often sans transition, to create a mood. But obscurity in poetry also comes into English through this poem. The still dominant notion of I-wrote-it-for-myself-and-don't-care-who-likes-it-so-there pose characterizing the true *artiste* was brought over from Eliot's imitating the French.

Eliot was far too conventional in his personal life to pose as a sulfur-breathing, absinthe-drinking Symbolist, but "The Waste Land" incorporates their fiercely nonmethodical methods—sordid characters and venues, lush music that aims for mood rather than meaning, a constantly shifting surface, free rein of private mythologies. I contend that if the writer is freed by Symbolist methods, so should the reader be. That means yielding to the poem in some way. Let it spray in your face, then wash over you.

Once you've absorbed the poem intuitively, feel free to crank up some scholarly interest. A decent anthology like the Norton will unpack every folded obscurity. Read the Baudelaire Eliot refers to. Listen to the Wagner. Just be forewarned that such investigations may not pay off with a different or greater understanding than your own reading will. You will get no encoded punchline unavailable from the poem's surface. You will ding no bell. So before you set off down that highway of inquiry, remember it's at your own volition more than the poem's, by my measure.

I fell in love with the poem in a small Texas town as a girl whose chief literary mark was her unabashed ignorance. In grad school, I learned to ape French and German and Latin pronunciations (the Greek's still Greek to me), and this adventure in music yielded up more than the scholarly rooting around I did whose artifacts were promptly forgotten. When I teach the poem, I have to look up many of the references every time. This amnesia of mine for the work's minuscule facts speaks volumes either to the doggedness of my afore-mentioned ignorance or to the trivial nature of said refer-ences. If you want to spend time doing background work, learning to pronounce the handful of foreign words seems more efficacious for tapping the poem's symphonic force, which is arguably its chief virtue.

But even as a girl, I found many of the poem's foreign quotes decipherable without knowing the language at hand. The Baudelaire line he steals is almost entirely lucid: "hyp-ocrite lecteur!—mon semblable,—mon frère!" I first read this as someone's accusing a lecturer of being a hypocrite—one of my favorite high school activities. I knew what *frère* meant from "Frère Jacques" and could also see the Latin root related to *similarity* buried in *semblable*—an intuition that lasted me for years before I took the initiative and a French dictionary to find it translated as *twin* and *lecteur* translated as *reader*. Only then did I twig to the irony of my being called a hypocrite who *resembles* to the point of replication the writer. Of course, the line means something different in actual rather than intuitive translation. But in some ways, the scornful tone of my mis-reading is not wholly inconsistent with the poet's. Also, the musical effect of the tone switch and the introduction of French come through even with my lunkheaded distortion. So while scholarly work might clarify, it often yields only a subtle change in flavor rather than a radically altered interpretation.

Lines 60 to 64 are just the sort that draw the microscopic attentions of people zeroing in for scholarly dissection:

> Unreal City,
> Under the brown fog of a winter dawn,
> A crowd flowed over London Bridge, so many,
> I had not thought death had undone so many.

Does it aid or alter the *meaning* of these lines to know that "Unreal City" is derived from Baudelaire's poem "The Seven

Old Men"? Or that Dante's *Inferno* depicts crowds of dead flowing in just such a manner? I don't think so.

In fact, to construct a bulky apparatus of scholarship over the poem can actually obscure it, throw its language out of balance. The two references to Baudelaire mentioned above (I'm referring also to that *hypocrite lecteur*) are comprised of eight words, two measly lines in a 433-line text. To dwell overmuch on their *meaning* is to dismantle the swift, non-rhetorical construct Eliot invented for the poem and our century. So while flipping your scholarly off switch, start to listen. That's much of what the poem is saying: Listen, goddamn it.

For music is the message. What you need to know is interwoven with the poem's melodies and dissonances. On the surface, the poem tells you everything. Take just one line: *"Under the brown fog of a winter dawn."* You can grasp that the fog's oppression makes the wintry scene bleaker without saying to yourself, *The fog's* above *the people where Heaven should be. At the turn of the century, people were abandoning traditional notions of Heaven. . . .* The noise of the lines is innately mournful. The image of people flowing over a bridge is further suggestive of faceless automatons, a mindlessly moving horde. When they abruptly become the dead (*"I had not thought death had undone so many"*), it's an apocryphal instant. You suddenly know that the realistic world you were observing is, in fact, a vision. The speaker's calm restraint in describing this awful scene is innately ironic, so that he embodies in a way the horror of alienation and emotional detachment. The imagery derives as much from the First War as from Dante. But again, neither reference gives you anything you wouldn't automatically get from the surface.

Although your listening to the poem doesn't have to be analytical—indeed shouldn't be—analysis can show how the music works on you unconsciously to evoke a feeling. The above passage is unified by humming *n* and *m* sounds (*uNder, browN, dawN, LoNdoN, MaNy, uNdoNe, Not, MaNy*). The short *u* sound set next to it is also slightly moaning in feel. A few words rhyme absolutely (*London, undone*); others are half off. This kind of imperfect, slightly discordant noise is associated with Modernism, which above all sought to stop poets from marching in lockstep.

To excerpt the poem is to tell lies about it, because so many different voices stream through it. Let me quote from two more passages in order to gesture at the poem's variety in diction and subject. Here, a neurotic wife is sitting in the parlor with her recalcitrant husband, who's refusal to speak is as aggressive as her whining insistence that he do so:

> 'Speak to me. Why do you never speak? Speak.
> 'What are you thinking of? What thinking? What?
> 'I never know what you are thinking. Think.'
>
> I think we are in rats' alley
> Where the dead men lost their bones.
>
> 'What is that noise?'
>   The wind under the door.
> 'What is that noise now? What is the wind doing?'
>   Nothing again nothing.

The starved sterility of the scene is again deadly because of its calm surface—irony again. The repetition tells you it's all replayed and often. And in 1922, this kind of regular use of domestic language in poetry was revolutionary.

Contrast this section with the pub scene in which one woman recounts how she urged another woman, Lil, to fix herself up before her man, Albert, returns from war:

> Now Albert's coming back, make yourself a bit smart.
> He'll want to know what you done with that money he gave
>   you
> To get yourself some teeth. He did, I was there.
> You have them all out, Lil, and get a nice set,

He said, I swear, I can't bear to look at you.
And no more can't I, I said, and think of poor Albert,
He's been in the army four years, he wants a good time,
And if you don't give it him, there's others will. . . .

This kind of squalid scene in poetry was also a radical departure from the norm—the woman with rotted teeth who can't bother to fix them, the suggested betrayal of the other women who'll entertain Albert unless Lil gets new dentures. Such raw diction and milieu was deemed unpoetic before Eliot though now the squalid is so ubiquitous as to seem hackneyed sometimes.

Other sections are more referential, yes. Just take the references and other aspects of the poem on blind faith. Read it first for joy. Shut up your head's claptrap and open yourself to fall in love with it. Treat it like a first date, which should begin with ignorance but also with hope. Only if you fall in love do you make a study of the beloved, for only passion lets us inquire into other people's mysteries with the vitality borne of conviction. With enough ardor, your date's off-putting manner of dismantling chicken becomes an adorable nuance. So it is with "The Waste Land."

The blossoming mind-states it induces are perhaps only available if you can turn off your analytical machinery long enough to embark on the poem's journey. Otherwise, you're like some passenger strapped into the shotgun seat nervously calculating mileage and trying to map the exact cant of the last hairpin turn while the caverns of hell whiz past and unnoticed flames lap against the glass.

But why read something so darkly despairing? And repeatedly? I mentioned its beauty before. But the poem also acts for me as a sort of vaccine against the horror it describes by injecting a nonlethal dosage of it. One can't get the same immunity by abstractly, willfully constructing a theory about the world and one's place in it. Theories are fine, but unfueled by feeling they remain gaseously theoretical. Few human beings can run very long on the fumes of an ideal. I begin each morning fairly intent on seizing the day and often abandon that wisdom with the first snapped shoelace. "The Waste Land" delivers a dose of feeling that enters you with a hard jolt. It changes you, for perhaps only passion can lend conviction to such a change.

If you're no stranger to such soul-paralyzing mind states as the poem creates, it may also serve as balm to the loneliness such states evoke by speaking out to your own hybrid species of spiritual pain.

In this way, it can work like the miracle of communion— you take the Eucharist of the writer's words into the rough meat of your body in order to be transformed by someone else's mysterious passion. It brings you into a community of like sufferers. There's healing in that, I think, despite the old Dale Carnegie wisdom that reading such stuff is a depressing wallow in the mud of one's own misery. I disagree. Having once kept an apartment in similarly barren regions to those in this poem, I return there now through art—or memory or premenstrual syndrome, or by intensely loving friends still stranded there. Reading the poem gives me the conviction to live my life, not with the despair and angst rendered, but with the alertness the poem demands. People spend hundreds of thousands of dollars in therapy for the same sense of presence in one's life, the same fusion of inner self and outer experience. The mere exercise of attention—eyes wide, ears pricked, heart open—is not a bad way to move through the world.

BIBLIOGRAPHY

Ackroyd, Peter. *T. S. Eliot: A Life.* New York: Simon & Schuster, 1984.

An Anthology of French Poetry from Nerval to Valéry in English Translation, edited by Angel Flores. New York: Doubleday Anchor Books, 1958.

Eliot, T. S. "The Use of Poetry and the Use of Criticism." In *Selected Prose of T. S. Eliot,* edited by Frank Kermode. New York: Harcourt Brace & Company, 1975.

———. "The Waste Land." In *T. S. Eliot Collected Poems 1909–1962.* New York: Harcourt Brace & Company, 1963.

Everdell, William R. *The First Moderns.* Chicago: University of Chicago Press, 1997.

Ezra Pound: American Odyssey. Produced, directed, and written by Lawrence Pitkethly. 1 hr. New York Center for Visual History, Inc., 1988. Film.

Gordon, Lyndall. *Eliot's Early Years.* New York: Oxford University Press, 1977.

Hough, Graham. *Selected Essays.* Cambridge: Cambridge University Press, 1980.

Hughes, Robert. *The Shock of the New.* New York: Alfred A. Knopf, 1980.

Jarrell, Randall. *No Other Book,* edited by Brad Leithauser. New York: HarperCollins Publishers, 1999.

———. "The Death of the Ball Turret Gunner." In *The Norton Anthology of Modern Poetry.* 2d ed. Edited by Richard Ellmann and Robert O'Clair. New York: W. W. Norton & Company, 1988.

Kenner, Hugh. *The Pound Era.* Berkeley: University of California Press, 1971.

Laughlin, James. *Remembering William Carlos Williams.* New York: New Directions, 1995.

Owen, Wilfred. "Dulce et Decorum Est." In *The Norton Introduction to Literature,* edited by J. Paul Hunter. W. W. Norton: New York, 1973.

Perkins, David. *A History of Modern Poetry: From the 1890s to the High Modernist Mode.* 2 vols. Cambridge, MA: Harvard University Press, 1976.

Pound, Ezra. *ABC of Reading.* New York: New Directions, 1934.

———. "A Few Don'ts by an Imagiste," *Poetry: A Magazine of Verse* 1, no. 1 (1912): 205.

———. *Selected Letters 1907–1941 of Ezra Pound,* edited by D. D. Paige. New York: New Directions, 1950.

Symons, Arthur. *The Symbolist Movement in Literature*. New York: E. P. Dutton and Co., Inc. 1958.

Van Doren, Charles. *A History of Knowledge*. New York: Ballantine Books, 1991.

————————

MARY KARR is an award-winning poet, essayist, and memoirist. She is the author of three books of poetry, *Abacus, The Devil's Tour,* and *Viper Rum,* and two memoirs, *The Liars' Club* and, most recently, *Cherry. The Liars' Club* won prizes for best first nonfiction from PEN (the Martha Albrand Award) and the Texas Institute of Letters. Her poems and essays have won Pushcart Prizes and have appeared in such magazines as *The New Yorker, The Atlantic,* and *Parnassus.* Her grants include the Whiting Award and the Bunting Fellowship from Radcliffe College. She is the Peck Professor of English Literature at Syracuse University.

THE WASTE LAND
AND
OTHER POEMS

PRUFROCK

AND OTHER OBSERVATIONS

1917

For Jean Verdenal, 1889–1915
mort aux Dardanelles

> *Or puoi la quantitate*
> *Comprender dell' amor ch'a te mi scalda,*
> *Quando dismento nostra vanitate*
> *Trattando l'ombre come cosa salda.*

THE LOVE SONG OF J. ALFRED PRUFROCK

> *S'io credesse che mia risposta fosse*
> *A persona che mai tornasse al mondo,*
> *Questa fiamma staria senza piu scosse.*
> *Ma perciocche giammai di questo fondo*
> *Non torno vivo alcun, s'i'odo il vero,*
> *Senza tema d'infamia ti rispondo.*

Let us go then, you and I,
When the evening is spread out against the sky
Like a patient etherised upon a table;
Let us go, through certain half-deserted streets,
The muttering retreats
Of restless nights in one-night cheap hotels
And sawdust restaurants with oyster-shells:

Streets that follow like a tedious argument
Of insidious intent
To lead you to an overwhelming question . . .
Oh, do not ask, "What is it?"
Let us go and make our visit.

In the room the women come and go
Talking of Michelangelo.

The yellow fog that rubs its back upon the window-panes,
The yellow smoke that rubs its muzzle on the window-panes
Licked its tongue into the corners of the evening,
Lingered upon the pools that stand in drains,
Let fall upon its back the soot that falls from chimneys,
Slipped by the terrace, made a sudden leap,
And seeing that it was a soft October night,
Curled once about the house, and fell asleep.

And indeed there will be time
For the yellow smoke that slides along the street,
Rubbing its back upon the window-panes;
There will be time, there will be time
To prepare a face to meet the faces that you meet;
There will be time to murder and create,
And time for all the works and days of hands
That lift and drop a question on your plate;
Time for you and time for me,
And time yet for a hundred indecisions,
And for a hundred visions and revisions,
Before the taking of a toast and tea.

In the room the women come and go
Talking of Michelangelo.

And indeed there will be time
To wonder, "Do I dare?" and, "Do I dare?"
Time to turn back and descend the stair,

With a bald spot in the middle of my hair—
[They will say: "How his hair is growing thin!"]
My morning coat, my collar mounting firmly to the chin,
My necktie rich and modest, but asserted by a simple pin—
[They will say: "But how his arms and legs are thin!"]
Do I dare
Disturb the universe?
In a minute there is time
For decisions and revisions which a minute will reverse.

For I have known them all already, known them all:—
Have known the evenings, mornings, afternoons,
I have measured out my life with coffee spoons;
I know the voices dying with a dying fall
Beneath the music from a farther room.
So how should I presume?

And I have known the eyes already, known them all—
The eyes that fix you in a formulated phrase,
And when I am formulated, sprawling on a pin,
When I am pinned and wriggling on the wall,
Then how should I begin
To spit out all the butt-ends of my days and ways?
And how should I presume?

And I have known the arms already, known them all—
Arms that are braceleted and white and bare
[But in the lamplight, downed with light brown hair!]
Is it perfume from a dress
That makes me so digress?
Arms that lie along a table, or wrap about a shawl.
And should I then presume?
And how should I begin?

.   .   .

Shall I say, I have gone at dusk through narrow streets
And watched the smoke that rises from the pipes
Of lonely men in shirt-sleeves, leaning out of windows? . . .

I should have been a pair of ragged claws
Scuttling across the floors of silent seas.

.   .   .

And the afternoon, the evening, sleeps so peacefully!
Smoothed by long fingers,
Asleep ... tired ... or it malingers,
Stretched on the floor, here beside you and me.
Should I, after tea and cakes and ices,
Have the strength to force the moment to its crisis?
But though I have wept and fasted, wept and prayed,
Though I have seen my head [grown slightly bald] brought
      in upon a platter,
I am no prophet—and here's no great matter;
I have seen the moment of my greatness flicker,
And I have seen the eternal Footman hold my coat, and
      snicker,
And in short, I was afraid.

And would it have been worth it, after all,
After the cups, the marmalade, the tea,
Among the porcelain, among some talk of you and me,
Would it have been worth while,
To have bitten off the matter with a smile,
To have squeezed the universe into a ball
To roll it toward some overwhelming question,
To say: "I am Lazarus, come from the dead,
Come back to tell you all, I shall tell you all"—
If one, settling a pillow by her head,
      Should say: "That is not what I meant at all.
      That is not it, at all."

And would it have been worth it, after all,
Would it have been worth while,
After the sunsets and the dooryards and the sprinkled streets,
After the novels, after the teacups, after the skirts that trail
      along the floor—

And this, and so much more?—
It is impossible to say just what I mean!
But as if a magic lantern threw the nerves in patterns on a
    screen:
Would it have been worth while
If one, settling a pillow or throwing off a shawl,
And turning toward the window, should say:
    "That is not it at all,
    That is not what I meant, at all."

No! I am not Prince Hamlet, nor was meant to be;
Am an attendant lord, one that will do
To swell a progress, start a scene or two,
Advise the prince; no doubt, an easy tool,
Deferential, glad to be of use,
Politic, cautious, and meticulous;
Full of high sentence, but a bit obtuse;
At times, indeed, almost ridiculous—
Almost, at times, the Fool.

I grow old . . . I grow old . . .
I shall wear the bottoms of my trousers rolled.

Shall I part my hair behind? Do I dare to eat a peach?
I shall wear white flannel trousers, and walk upon the beach.
I have heard the mermaids singing, each to each.

I do not think that they will sing to me.

I have seen them riding seaward on the waves
Combing the white hair of the waves blown back
When the wind blows the water white and black.

We have lingered in the chambers of the sea
By sea-girls wreathed with seaweed red and brown
Till human voices wake us, and we drown.

PORTRAIT OF A LADY

Thou hast committed—
Fornication: but that was in another country,
And besides, the wench is dead.

THE JEW OF MALTA.

I

Among the smoke and fog of a December afternoon
You have the scene arrange itself—as it will seem to do—
With "I have saved this afternoon for you";
And four wax candles in the darkened room,
Four rings of light upon the ceiling overhead,
An atmosphere of Juliet's tomb
Prepared for all the things to be said, or left unsaid.
We have been, let us say, to hear the latest Pole
Transmit the Preludes, through his hair and fingertips.
"So intimate, this Chopin, that I think his soul
Should be resurrected only among friends
Some two or three, who will not touch the bloom
That is rubbed and questioned in the concert room."
—And so the conversation slips
Among velleities and carefully caught regrets
Through attenuated tones of violins
Mingled with remote cornets
And begins.
"You do not know how much they mean to me, my friends,
And how, how rare and strange it is, to find
In a life composed so much, so much of odds and ends,
[For indeed I do not love it . . . you knew? you are not blind!
How keen you are!]
To find a friend who has these qualities,
Who has, and gives
Those qualities upon which friendship lives.
How much it means that I say this to you—
Without these friendships—life, what *cauchemar!*"

Among the windings of the violins
And the ariettes
Of cracked cornets
Inside my brain a dull tom-tom begins
Absurdly hammering a prelude of its own,
Capricious monotone
That is at least one definite "false note."
—Let us take the air, in a tobacco trance,
Admire the monuments,
Discuss the late events,
Correct our watches by the public clocks.
Then sit for half an hour and drink our bocks.

II

Now that lilacs are in bloom
She has a bowl of lilacs in her room
And twists one in her fingers while she talks.
"Ah, my friend, you do not know, you do not know
What life is, you who hold it in your hands";
(Slowly twisting the lilac stalks)
"You let it flow from you, you let it flow,
And youth is cruel, and has no remorse
And smiles at situations which it cannot see."
I smile, of course,
And go on drinking tea.
"Yet with these April sunsets, that somehow recall
My buried life, and Paris in the Spring,
I feel immeasurably at peace, and find the world
To be wonderful and youthful, after all."

The voice returns like the insistent out-of-tune
Of a broken violin on an August afternoon:
"I am always sure that you understand
My feelings, always sure that you feel,
Sure that across the gulf you reach your hand.

You are invulnerable, you have no Achilles' heel.
You will go on, and when you have prevailed
You can say: at this point many a one has failed.
But what have I, but what have I, my friend,
To give you, what can you receive from me?
Only the friendship and the sympathy
Of one about to reach her journey's end.

I shall sit here, serving tea to friends. . . ."

I take my hat: how can I make a cowardly amends
For what she has said to me?
You will see me any morning in the park
Reading the comics and the sporting page.
Particularly I remark
An English countess goes upon the stage.
A Greek was murdered at a Polish dance,
Another bank defaulter has confessed.
I keep my countenance,
I remain self-possessed
Except when a street piano, mechanical and tired
Reiterates some worn-out common song
With the smell of hyacinths across the garden
Recalling things that other people have desired.
Are these ideas right or wrong?

III

The October night comes down; returning as before
Except for a slight sensation of being ill at ease
I mount the stairs and turn the handle of the door
And feel as if I had mounted on my hands and knees.
"And so you are going abroad; and when do you return?
But that's a useless question.
You hardly know when you are coming back,
You will find so much to learn."
My smile falls heavily among the bric-à-brac.

"Perhaps you can write to me."
My self-possession flares up for a second;
This is as I had reckoned.
"I have been wondering frequently of late
(But our beginnings never know our ends!)
Why we have not developed into friends."
I feel like one who smiles, and turning shall remark
Suddenly, his expression in a glass.
My self-possession gutters; we are really in the dark.

"For everybody said so, all our friends,
They all were sure our feelings would relate
So closely! I myself can hardly understand.
We must leave it now to fate.
You will write, at any rate.
Perhaps it is not too late.
I shall sit here, serving tea to friends."

And I must borrow every changing shape
To find expression . . . dance, dance
Like a dancing bear,
Cry like a parrot, chatter like an ape.
Let us take the air, in a tobacco trance—

Well! and what if she should die some afternoon,
Afternoon grey and smoky, evening yellow and rose;
Should die and leave me sitting pen in hand
With the smoke coming down above the housetops;
Doubtful, for a while
Not knowing what to feel or if I understand
Or whether wise or foolish, tardy or too soon . . .
Would she not have the advantage, after all?
This music is successful with a "dying fall"
Now that we talk of dying—
And should I have the right to smile?

PRELUDES

I

The winter evening settles down
With smell of steaks in passageways.
Six o'clock.
The burnt-out ends of smoky days.
And now a gusty shower wraps
The grimy scraps
Of withered leaves about your feet
And newspapers from vacant lots;
The showers beat
On broken blinds and chimney-pots,
And at the corner of the street
A lonely cab-horse steams and stamps.
And then the lighting of the lamps.

II

The morning comes to consciousness
Of faint stale smells of beer
From the sawdust-trampled street
With all its muddy feet that press
To early coffee-stands.
With the other masquerades
That time resumes,
One thinks of all the hands
That are raising dingy shades
In a thousand furnished rooms.

III

You tossed a blanket from the bed,
You lay upon your back, and waited;
You dozed, and watched the night revealing
The thousand sordid images
Of which your soul was constituted;
They flickered against the ceiling.

And when all the world came back
And the light crept up between the shutters
And you heard the sparrows in the gutters,
You had such a vision of the street
As the street hardly understands;
Sitting along the bed's edge, where
You curled the papers from your hair,
Or clasped the yellow soles of feet
In the palms of both soiled hands.

IV

His soul stretched tight across the skies
That fade behind a city block,
Or trampled by insistent feet
At four and five and six o'clock;
And short square fingers stuffing pipes,
And evening newspapers, and eyes
Assured of certain certainties,
The conscience of a blackened street
Impatient to assume the world.

I am moved by fancies that are curled
Around these images, and cling:
The notion of some infinitely gentle
Infinitely suffering thing.

Wipe your hand across your mouth, and laugh;
The worlds revolve like ancient women
Gathering fuel in vacant lots.

RHAPSODY ON A WINDY NIGHT

Twelve o'clock.
Along the reaches of the street
Held in a lunar synthesis,
Whispering lunar incantations
Dissolve the floors of memory
And all its clear relations
Its divisions and precisions,
Every street lamp that I pass
Beats like a fatalistic drum,
And through the spaces of the dark
Midnight shakes the memory
As a madman shakes a dead geranium.

Half-past one,
The street-lamp sputtered,
The street-lamp muttered,
The street-lamp said, "Regard that woman
Who hesitates toward you in the light of the door
Which opens on her like a grin.
You see the border of her dress
Is torn and stained with sand,
And you see the corner of her eye
Twists like a crooked pin."

The memory throws up high and dry
A crowd of twisted things,
A twisted branch upon the beach
Eaten smooth, and polished
As if the world gave up
The secret of its skeleton,
Stiff and white.
A broken spring in a factory yard,
Rust that clings to the form that the strength has left
Hard and curled and ready to snap.

Half-past two,
The street-lamp said,
"Remark the cat which flattens itself in the gutter,
Slips out its tongue
And devours a morsel of rancid butter."
So the hand of the child, automatic,
Slipped out and pocketed a toy that was running along the
        quay.
I could see nothing behind that child's eye.
I have seen eyes in the street
Trying to peer through lighted shutters,
And a crab one afternoon in a pool,
An old crab with barnacles on his back,
Gripped the end of a stick which I held him.

    Half-past three,
The lamp sputtered,
The lamp muttered in the dark.
The lamp hummed:
"Regard the moon,
La lune ne garde aucune rancune,
She winks a feeble eye,
She smiles into corners.
She smooths the hair of the grass.
The moon has lost her memory.
A washed-out smallpox cracks her face,
Her hand twists a paper rose,
That smells of dust and eau de Cologne,
She is alone
With all the old nocturnal smells
That cross and cross across her brain."
The reminiscence comes
Of sunless dry geraniums
And dust in crevices,
Smells of chestnuts in the streets,

And female smells in shuttered rooms,
And cigarettes in corridors
And cocktail smells in bars.

    The lamp said,
"Four o'clock,
Here is the number on the door.
Memory!
You have the key,
The little lamp spreads a ring on the stair.
Mount.
The bed is open; the tooth-brush hangs on the wall,
Put your shoes at the door, sleep, prepare for life."

    The last twist of the knife.

MORNING AT THE WINDOW

They are rattling breakfast plates in basement kitchens,
And along the trampled edges of the street
I am aware of the damp souls of housemaids
Sprouting despondently at area gates.

    The brown waves of fog toss up to me
Twisted faces from the bottom of the street,
And tear from a passer-by with muddy skirts
An aimless smile that hovers in the air
And vanishes along the level of the roofs.

THE *BOSTON EVENING TRANSCRIPT*

The readers of the *Boston Evening Transcript*
Sway in the wind like a field of ripe corn.

    When evening quickens faintly in the street,
Wakening the appetites of life in some

And to others bringing the *Boston Evening Transcript*,
I mount the steps and ring the bell, turning
Wearily, as one would turn to nod good-bye to
      Rochefoucauld,
If the street were time and he at the end of the street,
And I say, "Cousin Harriet, here is the *Boston Evening
      Transcript.*"

AUNT HELEN

Miss Helen Slingsby was my maiden aunt,
And lived in a small house near a fashionable square
Cared for by servants to the number of four.
Now when she died there was silence in heaven
And silence at her end of the street.
The shutters were drawn and the undertaker wiped his feet—
He was aware that this sort of thing had occurred before.
The dogs were handsomely provided for,
But shortly afterwards the parrot died too.
The Dresden clock continued ticking on the mantelpiece,
And the footman sat upon the dining-table
Holding the second housemaid on his knees—
Who had always been so careful while her mistress lived.

COUSIN NANCY

Miss Nancy Ellicott
Strode across the hills and broke them,
Rode across the hills and broke them—
The barren New England hills—
Riding to hounds
Over the cow-pasture.

    Miss Nancy Ellicott smoked
And danced all the modern dances;

And her aunts were not quite sure how they felt about it,
But they knew that it was modern.
    Upon the glazen shelves kept watch
Matthew and Waldo, guardians of the faith,
The army of unalterable law.

MR. APOLLINAX

Ω τῆς καινότητος. Ἡράκλεις, τῆς παραδοξολογίας.
εὐμήχανος ἄνθρωπος.

LUCIAN.

When Mr. Apollinax visited the United States
His laughter tinkled among the teacups.
I thought of Fragilion, that shy figure among the birch-
    trees,
And of Priapus in the shrubbery
Gaping at the lady in the swing.
In the palace of Mrs. Phlaccus, at Professor Channing-
    Cheetah's
He laughed like an irresponsible fœtus.
His laughter was submarine and profound
Like the old man of the sea's
Hidden under coral islands
Where worried bodies of drowned men drift down in the
    green silence,
Dropping from fingers of surf.
I looked for the head of Mr. Apollinax rolling under a
    chair.

    Or grinning over a screen
With seaweed in its hair.
I heard the beat of centaur's hoofs over the hard turf
As his dry and passionate talk devoured the afternoon.

"He is a charming man"—"But after all what did he
      mean?"—
"His pointed ears. . . . He must be unbalanced,"—
"There was something he said that I might have challenged."
Of dowager Mrs. Phlaccus, and Professor and Mrs.
      Cheetah
I remember a slice of lemon, and a bitten macaroon.

HYSTERIA

As she laughed I was aware of becoming involved in her
laughter and being part of it, until her teeth were only acci-
dental stars with a talent for squad-drill. I was drawn in by
short gasps, inhaled at each momentary recovery, lost finally
in the dark caverns of her throat, bruised by the ripple of un-
seen muscles. An elderly waiter with trembling hands was
hurriedly spreading a pink and white checked cloth over the
rusty green iron table, saying: "If the lady and gentleman
wish to take their tea in the garden, if the lady and gentleman
wish to take their tea in the garden . . ." I decided that if the
shaking of her breasts could be stopped, some of the frag-
ments of the afternoon might be collected, and I concen-
trated my attention with careful subtlety to this end.

CONVERSATION GALANTE

I observe: "Our sentimental friend the moon!
Or possibly (fantastic, I confess)
It may be Prester John's balloon
Or an old battered lantern hung aloft
To light poor travellers to their distress."
      She then: "How you digress!"

And I then: "Someone frames upon the keys
That exquisite nocturne, with which we explain
The night and moonshine; music which we seize
To body forth our own vacuity."
    She then: "Does this refer to me?"
"Oh no, it is I who am inane."

"You, madam, are the eternal humorist,
The eternal enemy of the absolute,
Giving our vagrant moods the slightest twist!
With your air indifferent and imperious
At a stroke our mad poetics to confute—"
    And—"Are we then so serious?"

LA FIGLIA CHE PIANGE

O quam te memorem virgo . . .

Stand on the highest pavement of the stair—
Lean on a garden urn—
Weave, weave the sunlight in your hair—
Clasp your flowers to you with a pained surprise—
Fling them to the ground and turn
With a fugitive resentment in your eyes:
But weave, weave the sunlight in your hair.

    So I would have had him leave,
So I would have had her stand and grieve,
So he would have left
As the soul leaves the body torn and bruised,
As the mind deserts the body it has used.
I should find
Some way incomparably light and deft,
Some way we both should understand,
Simple and faithless as a smile and shake of the hand.

She turned away, but with the autumn weather
Compelled my imagination many days,
Many days and many hours:
Her hair over her arms and her arms full of flowers.
And I wonder how they should have been together!
I should have lost a gesture and a pose.
Sometimes these cogitations still amaze
The troubled midnight and the noon's repose.

POEMS
1920

GERONTION

Thou hast nor youth nor age
But as it were an after dinner sleep
Dreaming of both.

Here I am, an old man in a dry month,
Being read to by a boy, waiting for rain.
I was neither at the hot gates
Nor fought in the warm rain
Nor knee deep in the salt marsh, heaving a cutlass,
Bitten by flies, fought.
My house is a decayed house,
And the jew squats on the window sill, the owner,
Spawned in some estaminet of Antwerp,
Blistered in Brussels, patched and peeled in London.
The goat coughs at night in the field overhead;
Rocks, moss, stonecrop, iron, merds.
The woman keeps the kitchen, makes tea,
Sneezes at evening, poking the peevish gutter.
                                   I an old man,
A dull head among windy spaces.

   Signs are taken for wonders. "We would see a sign!"
The word within a word, unable to speak a word,

Swaddled with darkness. In the juvescence of the year
Came Christ the tiger

In depraved May, dogwood and chestnut, flowering judas,
To be eaten, to be divided, to be drunk
Among whispers; by Mr. Silvero
With caressing hands, at Limoges
Who walked all night in the next room;

By Hakagawa, bowing among the Titians;
By Madame de Tornquist, in the dark room
Shifting the candles; Fräulein von Kulp
Who turned in the hall, one hand on the door.
        Vacant shuttles
Weave the wind. I have no ghosts,
An old man in a draughty house
Under a windy knob.

After such knowledge, what forgiveness? Think now
History has many cunning passages, contrived corridors
And issues, deceives with whispering ambitions,
Guides us by vanities. Think now
She gives when our attention is distracted
And what she gives, gives with such supple confusions
That the giving famishes the craving. Gives too late
What's not believed in, or if still believed,
In memory only, reconsidered passion. Gives too soon
Into weak hands, what's thought can be dispensed with
Till the refusal propagates a fear. Think
Neither fear nor courage saves us. Unnatural vices
Are fathered by our heroism. Virtues
Are forced upon us by our impudent crimes.
These tears are shaken from the wrath-bearing tree.

The tiger springs in the new year. Us he devours. Think
        at last
We have not reached conclusion, when I
Stiffen in a rented house. Think at last

I have not made this show purposelessly
And it is not by any concitation
Of the backward devils.
I would meet you upon this honestly.
I that was near your heart was removed therefrom
To lose beauty in terror, terror in inquisition.
I have lost my passion: why should I need to keep it
Since what is kept must be adulterated?
I have lost my sight, smell, hearing, taste and touch:
How should I use them for your closer contact?

These with a thousand small deliberations
Protract the profit of their chilled delirium,
Excite the membrane, when the sense has cooled,
With pungent sauces, multiply variety
In a wilderness of mirrors. What will the spider do,
Suspend its operations, will the weevil
Delay? De Bailhache, Fresca, Mrs. Cammel, whirled
Beyond the circuit of the shuddering Bear
In fractured atoms. Gull against the wind, in the windy
    straits
Of Belle Isle, or running on the Horn,
White feathers in the snow, the Gulf claims,
And an old man driven by the Trades
To a sleepy corner.

                Tenants of the house,
Thoughts of a dry brain in a dry season.

BURBANK WITH A BAEDEKER:
BLEISTEIN WITH A CIGAR

Tra-la-la-la-la-la-laire—nil nisi divinum stabile est; caetera fumus—the gondola stopped, the old palace was there, how charming its grey and pink—goats and monkeys, with such hair too!—so the countess passed on until she came through the little park, where Niobe presented her with a cabinet, and so departed.

Burbank crossed a little bridge
    Descending at a small hotel;
Princess Volupine arrived,
    They were together, and he fell.

Defunctive music under sea
    Passed seaward with the passing bell
Slowly: the God Hercules
    Had left him, that had loved him well.

The horses, under the axletree
    Beat up the dawn from Istria
With even feet. Her shuttered barge
    Burned on the water all the day.

But this or such was Bleistein's way:
    A saggy bending of the knees
And elbows, with the palms turned out,
    Chicago Semite Viennese.

A lustreless protrusive eye
    Stares from the protozoic slime
At a perspective of Canaletto.
    The smoky candle end of time

Declines. On the Rialto once.
    The rats are underneath the piles.
The jew is underneath the lot.
    Money in furs. The boatman smiles,

Princess Volupine extends
    A meagre, blue-nailed, phthisic hand
To climb the waterstair. Lights, lights,
    She entertains Sir Ferdinand

Klein. Who clipped the lion's wings
    And flea'd his rump and pared his claws?
Thought Burbank, meditating on
    Time's ruins, and the seven laws.

SWEENEY ERECT

And the trees about me,
Let them be dry and leafless; let the rocks
Groan with continual surges; and behind me
Make all a desolation. Look, look, wenches!

Paint me a cavernous waste shore
    Cast in the unstilled Cyclades,
Paint me the bold anfractuous rocks
    Faced by the snarled and yelping seas.

Display me Aeolus above
    Reviewing the insurgent gales
Which tangle Ariadne's hair
    And swell with haste the perjured sails.

Morning stirs the feet and hands
    (Nausicaa and Polypheme).
Gesture of orang-outang
    Rises from the sheets in steam.

This withered root of knots of hair
    Slitted below and gashed with eyes,
This oval O cropped out with teeth:
    The sickle motion from the thighs

Jackknifes upward at the knees
    Then straightens out from heel to hip
Pushing the framework of the bed
    And clawing at the pillow slip.

Sweeney addressed full length to shave
    Broadbottomed, pink from nape to base,
Knows the female temperament
    And wipes the suds around his face.

(The lengthened shadow of a man
    Is history, said Emerson
Who had not seen the silhouette
    Of Sweeney straddled in the sun.)

Tests the razor on his leg
    Waiting until the shriek subsides.
The epileptic on the bed
    Curves backward, clutching at her sides.

The ladies of the corridor
    Find themselves involved, disgraced,
Call witness to their principles
    And deprecate the lack of taste

Observing that hysteria
    Might easily be misunderstood;
Mrs. Turner intimates
    It does the house no sort of good.

But Doris, towelled from the bath,
    Enters padding on broad feet,
Bringing sal volatile
    And a glass of brandy neat.

A COOKING EGG

En l'an trentiesme de mon aage
Que toutes mes hontes j'ay beues . . .

Pipit sate upright in her chair
    Some distance from where I was sitting;
Views of the Oxford Colleges
    Lay on the table, with the knitting.

Daguerreotypes and silhouettes,
    Her grandfather and great great aunts,
Supported on the mantelpiece
    An *Invitation to the Dance.*

    ·   ·   ·

I shall not want Honour in Heaven
    For I shall meet Sir Philip Sidney
And have talk with Coriolanus
    And other heroes of that kidney.

I shall not want Capital in Heaven
    For I shall meet Sir Alfred Mond.
We two shall lie together, lapt
    In a five per cent. Exchequer Bond.

I shall not want Society in Heaven,
    Lucretia Borgia shall be my Bride;
Her anecdotes will be more amusing
    Than Pipit's experience could provide.

I shall not want Pipit in Heaven:
    Madame Blavatsky will instruct me
In the Seven Sacred Trances;
    Piccarda de Donati will conduct me.

    ·   ·   ·

But where is the penny world I bought
    To eat with Pipit behind the screen?

The red-eyed scavengers are creeping
    From Kentish Town and Golder's Green;

Where are the eagles and the trumpets?

    Buried beneath some snow-deep Alps.
Over buttered scones and crumpets
    Weeping, weeping multitudes
Droop in a hundred A.B.C.'s

LE DIRECTEUR

Malheur à la malheureuse Tamise
Qui coule si près du Spectateur.
Le directeur
Conservateur
Du Spectateur
Empeste la brise.
Les actionnaires
Réactionnaires
Du Spectateur
Conservateur
Bras dessus bras dessous
Font des tours
A pas de loup.
Dans un égout
Une petite fille
En guenilles
Camarde
Regarde
Le directeur
Du Spectateur
Conservateur
Et crève d'amour.

Mélange Adultere de Tout

En Amérique, professeur;
En Angleterre, journaliste;
C'est à grands pas et en sueur
Que vous suivrez à peine ma piste.
En Yorkshire, conférencier;
A Londres, un peu banquier,
Vous me paierez bien la tête.
C'est à Paris que je me coiffe
Casque noir de jemenfoutiste.
En Allemagne, philosophe
Surexcité par Emporheben
Au grand air de Bergsteigleben;
J'erre toujours de-ci de-là
A divers coups de tra là là
De Damas jusqu'à Omaha.
Je célébrai mon jour de fête
Dans une oasis d'Afrique
Vetu d'une peau de girafe.

On montrera mon cénotaphe
Aux côtes brulantes de Mozambique.

Lune de Miel

Ils ont vu les Pays-Bas, ils rentrent à Terre Haute;
Mais une nuit d'été, les voici à Ravenne,
A l'aise entre deux draps, chez deux centaines de punaises;
La sueur aestivale, et une forte odeur de chienne.
Ils restent sur le dos écartant les genoux
De quatre jambes molles tout gonflées de morsures.
On relève le drap pour mieux égratigner.
Moins d'une lieue d'ici est Saint Apollinaire
En Classe, basilique connue des amateurs
De chapitaux d'acanthe que tournoie le vent.

Ils vont prendre le train de huit heures
Prolonger leurs misères de Padoue à Milan
Où se trouvent la Cène, et un restaurant pas cher.
Lui pense aux pourboires, et rédige son bilan.
Ils auront vu la Suisse et traversé la France.
Et Saint Apollinaire, raide et ascétique,
Vieille usine désaffectée de Dieu, tient encore
Dans ses pierres écroulantes la forme précise de Byzance.

THE HIPPOPOTAMUS

Similiter et omnes revereantur Diaconos, ut mandatum Jesu Christi; et Episcopum, ut Jesum Christum, existentem filium Patris; Presbyteros autem, ut concilium Dei et conjunctionem Apostolorum. Sine his Ecclesia non vocatur; de quibus suadeo vos sic habeo.

S. IGNATII AD TRALLIANOS.

And when this epistle is read among you, cause that it be read also in the church of the Laodiceans.

The broad-backed hippopotamus
Rests on his belly in the mud;
Although he seems so firm to us
He is merely flesh and blood.

Flesh and blood is weak and frail,
Susceptible to nervous shock;
While the True Church can never fail
For it is based upon a rock.

The hippo's feeble steps may err
In compassing material ends,
While the True Church need never stir
To gather in its dividends.

The 'potamus can never reach
The mango on the mango-tree;

But fruits of pomegranate and peach
Refresh the Church from over sea.

At mating time the hippo's voice
Betrays inflexions hoarse and odd,
But every week we hear rejoice
The Church, at being one with God.

The hippopotamus's day
Is passed in sleep; at night he hunts;
God works in a mysterious way—
The Church can sleep and feed at once.

I saw the 'potamus take wing
Ascending from the damp savannas,
And quiring angels round him sing
The praise of God, in loud hosannas.

Blood of the Lamb shall wash him clean
And him shall heavenly arms enfold,
Among the saints he shall be seen
Performing on a harp of gold.

He shall be washed as white as snow,
By all the martyr'd virgins kist,
While the True Church remains below
Wrapt in the old miasmal mist.

DANS LE RESTAURANT

Le garçon délabré qui n'a rien à faire
Que de se gratter les doigts et se pencher sur mon épaule:
"Dans mon pays il fera temps pluvieux,
Du vent, du grand soleil, et de la pluie;
C'est ce qu'on appelle le jour de lessive des gueux."
(Bavard, baveux, à la croupe arrondie,
Je te prie, au moins, ne bave pas dans la soupe.)

"Les saules trempés, et des bourgeons sur les ronces—
C'est là, dans une averse, qu'on s'abrite.
J'avais sept ans, elle était plus petite.
    Elle était toute mouillée, je lui ai donné des
        primevères."
Les taches de son gilet montent au chiffre de trente-huit.
    "Je la chatouillais, pour la faire rire.
    J'éprouvais un instant de puissance et de délire."
    Mais alors, vieux lubrique, à cet âge . . .
"Monsieur, le fait est dur.
    Il est venu, nous peloter, un gros chien;
    Moi j'avais peur, je l'ai quittée à mi-chemin.
    C'est dommage."
        Mais alors, tu as ton vautour!

Va t'en te décrotter les rides du visage;
Tiens, ma fourchette, décrasse-toi le crâne.
De quel droit payes-tu des expériences comme moi?
Tiens, voilà dix sous, pour la salle-de-bains.

    Phlébas, le Phénicien, pendant quinze jours noyé,
Oubliait les cris des mouettes et la houle de Cornouaille,
Et les profits et les pertes, et la cargaison d'étain:
Un courant de sous-mer l'emporta très loin,
Le repassant aux étapes de sa vie antérieure.
Figurez-vous donc, c'était un sort pénible;
Cependant, ce fut jadis un bel homme, de haute taille.

WHISPERS OF IMMORTALITY

Webster was much possessed by death
And saw the skull beneath the skin;
And breastless creatures under ground
Leaned backward with a lipless grin.

    Daffodil bulbs instead of balls
Stared from the sockets of the eyes!

He knew that thought clings round dead limbs
Tightening its lusts and luxuries.

Donne, I suppose, was such another
Who found no substitute for sense,
To seize and clutch and penetrate;
Expert beyond experience,

He knew the anguish of the marrow
The ague of the skeleton;
No contact possible to flesh
Allayed the fever of the bone.

.   .   .

Grishkin is nice: her Russian eye
Is underlined for emphasis;
Uncorseted, her friendly bust
Gives promise of pneumatic bliss.

The couched Brazilian jaguar
Compels the scampering marmoset
With subtle effluence of cat;
Grishkin has a maisonette;

The sleek Brazilian jaguar
Does not in its arboreal gloom
Distil so rank a feline smell
As Grishkin in a drawing-room.

And even the Abstract Entities
Circumambulate her charm;
But our lot crawls between dry ribs
To keep our metaphysics warm.

MR. ELIOT'S SUNDAY MORNING SERVICE

Look, look, master, here comes two religious caterpillars.
THE JEW OF MALTA.

Polyphiloprogenitive
The sapient sutlers of the Lord
Drift across the window-panes.
In the beginning was the Word.

In the beginning was the Word.
Superfetation of τὸ ἕν,
And at the mensual turn of time
Produced enervate Origen.

A painter of the Umbrian school
Designed upon a gesso ground
The nimbus of the Baptized God.
The wilderness is cracked and browned

But through the water pale and thin
Still shine the unoffending feet
And there above the painter set
The Father and the Paraclete.

.   .   .

The sable presbyters approach
The avenue of penitence;
The young are red and pustular
Clutching piaculative pence.

Under the penitential gates
Sustained by staring Seraphim
Where the souls of the devout
Burn invisible and dim.

Along the garden-wall the bees
With hairy bellies pass between
The staminate and pistilate,
Blest office of the epicene.

Sweeney shifts from ham to ham
Stirring the water in his bath.
The masters of the subtle schools
Are controversial, polymath.

SWEENEY AMONG THE NIGHTINGALES

ὤμοι, πέπληγμαι καιρίαν πληγὴν ἔσω.

Apeneck Sweeney spreads his knees
Letting his arms hang down to laugh,
The zebra stripes along his jaw
Swelling to maculate giraffe.

The circles of the stormy moon
Slide westward toward the River Plate,
Death and the Raven drift above
And Sweeney guards the hornèd gate.

Gloomy Orion and the Dog
Are veiled; and hushed the shrunken seas;
The person in the Spanish cape
Tries to sit on Sweeney's knees

Slips and pulls the table cloth
Overturns a coffee-cup,
Reorganized upon the floor
She yawns and draws a stocking up;

The silent man in mocha brown
Sprawls at the window-sill and gapes;
The waiter brings in oranges
Bananas figs and hothouse grapes;

The silent vertebrate in brown
Contracts and concentrates, withdraws;

Rachel *née* Rabinovitch
Tears at the grapes with murderous paws;

She and the lady in the cape
Are suspect, thought to be in league;
Therefore the man with heavy eyes
Declines the gambit, shows fatigue,

Leaves the room and reappears
Outside the window, leaning in,
Branches of wistaria
Circumscribe a golden grin;

The host with someone indistinct
Converses at the door apart,
The nightingales are singing near
The Convent of the Sacred Heart,

And sang within the bloody wood
When Agamemnon cried aloud,
And let their liquid siftings fall
To stain the stiff dishonoured shroud.

The Waste Land
1922

"Nam Sibyllam quidem Cumis ego ipse oculis meis vidi in ampulla pendere, et cum illi pueri dicerent: Σίβυλλα τί θέλεις; *respondebat illa:* ἀποθανεῖν θέλω."*

For Ezra Pound
il miglior fabbro.

I. The Burial of the Dead

April is the cruellest month, breeding
Lilacs out of the dead land, mixing
Memory and desire, stirring
Dull roots with spring rain.
Winter kept us warm, covering
Earth in forgetful snow, feeding
A little life with dried tubers.
Summer surprised us, coming over the Starnbergersee
With a shower of rain; we stopped in the colonnade,
And went on in sunlight, into the Hofgarten,   10
And drank coffee, and talked for an hour.
Bin gar keine Russin, stamm' aus Litauen, echt deutsch.
And when we were children, staying at the archduke's,
My cousin's, he took me out on a sled,
And I was frightened. He said, Marie,
Marie, hold on tight. And down we went.
In the mountains, there you feel free.
I read, much of the night, and go south in the winter.

    What are the roots that clutch, what branches grow
Out of this stony rubbish? Son of man,   20

You cannot say, or guess, for you know only
A heap of broken images, where the sun beats,
And the dead tree gives no shelter, the cricket no relief,
And the dry stone no sound of water. Only
There is shadow under this red rock,
(Come in under the shadow of this red rock),
And I will show you something different from either
Your shadow at morning striding behind you
Or your shadow at evening rising to meet you;
I will show you fear in a handful of dust.   30

>   *Frisch weht der Wind*
>   *Der Heimat zu*
>   *Mein Irisch Kind,*
>   *Wo weilest du?*

"You gave me hyacinths first a year ago;
"They called me the hyacinth girl."
—Yet when we came back, late, from the Hyacinth garden,
Your arms full, and your hair wet, I could not
Speak, and my eyes failed, I was neither
Living nor dead, and I knew nothing,   40
Looking into the heart of light, the silence.
Oed' und leer das Meer.

Madame Sosostris, famous clairvoyante,
Had a bad cold, nevertheless
Is known to be the wisest woman in Europe,
With a wicked pack of cards. Here, said she,
Is your card, the drowned Phoenician Sailor,
(Those are pearls that were his eyes. Look!)
Here is Belladonna, the Lady of the Rocks,
The lady of situations.   50
Here is the man with three staves, and here the Wheel,
And here is the one-eyed merchant, and this card,
Which is blank, is something he carries on his back,
Which I am forbidden to see. I do not find
The Hanged Man. Fear death by water.

I see crowds of people, walking round in a ring.
Thank you. If you see dear Mrs. Equitone,
Tell her I bring the horoscope myself:
One must be so careful these days.

    Unreal City,   60
Under the brown fog of a winter dawn,
A crowd flowed over London Bridge, so many,
I had not thought death had undone so many.
Sighs, short and infrequent, were exhaled,
And each man fixed his eyes before his feet.
Flowed up the hill and down King William Street,
To where Saint Mary Woolnoth kept the hours
With a dead sound on the final stroke of nine.
There I saw one I knew, and stopped him, crying: "Stetson!
"You who were with me in the ships at Mylae!   70
"That corpse you planted last year in your garden,
"Has it begun to sprout? Will it bloom this year?
"Or has the sudden frost disturbed its bed?
"Oh keep the Dog far hence, that's friend to men,
"Or with his nails he'll dig it up again!
"You! hypocrite lecteur!—mon semblable,—mon frère!"

II. A GAME OF CHESS

The Chair she sat in, like a burnished throne,
Glowed on the marble, where the glass
Held up by standards wrought with fruited vines   80
From which a golden Cupidon peeped out
(Another hid his eyes behind his wing)
Doubled the flames of sevenbranched candelabra
Reflecting light upon the table as
The glitter of her jewels rose to meet it,
From satin cases poured in rich profusion;
In vials of ivory and coloured glass

Unstoppered, lurked her strange synthetic perfumes,
Unguent, powdered, or liquid—troubled, confused
And drowned the sense in odours; stirred by the air
That freshened from the window, these ascended   90
In fattening the prolonged candle-flames,
Flung their smoke into the laquearia,
Stirring the pattern on the coffered ceiling.
Huge sea-wood fed with copper
Burned green and orange, framed by the coloured stone,
In which sad light a carvèd dolphin swam.
Above the antique mantel was displayed
As though a window gave upon the sylvan scene
The change of Philomel, by the barbarous king
So rudely forced; yet there the nightingale   100
Filled all the desert with inviolable voice
And still she cried, and still the world pursues,
"Jug Jug" to dirty ears.
And other withered stumps of time
Were told upon the walls; staring forms
Leaned out, leaning, hushing the room enclosed.
Footsteps shuffled on the stair.
Under the firelight, under the brush, her hair
Spread out in fiery points
Glowed into words, then would be savagely still.   110

    "My nerves are bad to-night. Yes, bad. Stay with me.
"Speak to me. Why do you never speak. Speak.
    "What are you thinking of? What thinking? What?
"I never know what you are thinking. Think."

    I think we are in rats' alley
Where the dead men lost their bones.

    "What is that noise?"
                        The wind under the door.
"What is that noise now? What is the wind doing?"
                        Nothing again nothing.   120

                    "Do
"You know nothing? Do you see nothing? Do you remember
"Nothing?"

     I remember
Those are pearls that were his eyes.
"Are you alive, or not? Is there nothing in your head?"

                    But

O O O O that Shakespeherian Rag—
It's so elegant
So intelligent   130
"What shall I do now? What shall I do?"
"I shall rush out as I am, and walk the street
"With my hair down, so. What shall we do to-morrow?
"What shall we ever do?"

             The hot water at ten.
And if it rains, a closed car at four.
And we shall play a game of chess,
Pressing lidless eyes and waiting for a knock upon the
     door.

     When Lil's husband got demobbed, I said—
I didn't mince my words, I said to her myself,   140
HURRY UP PLEASE ITS TIME
Now Albert's coming back, make yourself a bit smart.
He'll want to know what you done with that money he
     gave you
To get yourself some teeth. He did, I was there.
You have them all out, Lil, and get a nice set,
He said, I swear, I can't bear to look at you.
And no more can't I, I said, and think of poor Albert,
He's been in the army four years, he wants a good time,
And if you don't give it him, there's others will, I said.
Oh is there, she said. Something o' that, I said.   150
Then I'll know who to thank, she said, and give me a
     straight look.

HURRY UP PLEASE ITS TIME
If you don't like it you can get on with it, I said.
Others can pick and choose if you can't.
But if Albert makes off, it won't be for lack of telling.
You ought to be ashamed, I said, to look so antique.
(And her only thirty-one.)
I can't help it, she said, pulling a long face,
It's them pills I took, to bring it off, she said.
(She's had five already, and nearly died of young
      George.)   160
The chemist said it would be all right, but I've never been
      the same.
You are a proper fool, I said.
Well, if Albert won't leave you alone, there it is, I said,
What you get married for if you don't want children?
HURRY UP PLEASE ITS TIME
Well, that Sunday Albert was home, they had a hot gammon,
And they asked me in to dinner, to get the beauty of it hot—
HURRY UP PLEASE ITS TIME
HURRY UP PLEASE ITS TIME
Goonight Bill. Goonight Lou. Goonight May.
      Goonight.   170
Ta ta. Goonight. Goonight.
Good night, ladies, good night, sweet ladies, good night,
      good night.

III. THE FIRE SERMON

The river's tent is broken: the last fingers of leaf
Clutch and sink into the wet bank. The wind
Crosses the brown land, unheard. The nymphs are
      departed.
Sweet Thames, run softly, till I end my song.
The river bears no empty bottles, sandwich papers,

Silk handkerchiefs, cardboard boxes, cigarette ends
Or other testimony of summer nights. The nymphs are
    departed.
And their friends, the loitering heirs of city directors;   180
Departed, have left no addresses.
By the waters of Leman I sat down and wept . . .
Sweet Thames, run softly till I end my song,
Sweet Thames, run softly, for I speak not loud or long.
But at my back in a cold blast I hear
The rattle of the bones, and chuckle spread from ear to ear.
A rat crept softly through the vegetation
Dragging its slimy belly on the bank
While I was fishing in the dull canal
On a winter evening round behind the gashouse   190
Musing upon the king my brother's wreck
And on the king my father's death before him.
White bodies naked on the low damp ground
And bones cast in a little low dry garret,
Rattled by the rat's foot only, year to year.
But at my back from time to time I hear
The sound of horns and motors, which shall bring
Sweeney to Mrs. Porter in the spring.
O the moon shone bright on Mrs. Porter
And on her daughter   200
They wash their feet in soda water
Et O ces voix d'enfants, chantant dans la coupole!

    Twit twit twit
Jug jug jug jug jug jug
So rudely forc'd.
Tereu

    Unreal City
Under the brown fog of a winter noon
Mr. Eugenides, the Smyrna merchant
Unshaven, with a pocket full of currants   210
C.i.f. London: documents at sight,

Asked me in demotic French
To luncheon at the Cannon Street Hotel
Followed by a weekend at the Metropole.

　　At the violet hour, when the eyes and back
Turn upward from the desk, when the human engine waits
Like a taxi throbbing waiting,
I Tiresias, though blind, throbbing between two lives,
Old man with wrinkled female breasts, can see
At the violet hour, the evening hour that strives　　　　220
Homeward, and brings the sailor home from sea,
The typist home at teatime, clears her breakfast, lights
Her stove, and lays out food in tins.
Out of the window perilously spread
Her drying combinations touched by the sun's last rays,
On the divan are piled (at night her bed)
Stockings, slippers, camisoles, and stays.
I Tiresias, old man with wrinkled dugs
Perceived the scene, and foretold the rest—
I too awaited the expected guest.　　　　230
He, the young man carbuncular, arrives,
A small house agent's clerk, with one bold stare,
One of the low on whom assurance sits
As a silk hat on a Bradford millionaire.
The time is now propitious, as he guesses,
The meal is ended, she is bored and tired,
Endeavours to engage her in caresses
Which still are unreproved, if undesired.
Flushed and decided, he assaults at once;
Exploring hands encounter no defence;　　　　240
His vanity requires no response,
And makes a welcome of indifference.
(And I Tiresias have foresuffered all
Enacted on this same divan or bed;
I who have sat by Thebes below the wall
And walked among the lowest of the dead.)

Bestows one final patronising kiss,
And gropes his way, finding the stairs unlit . . .

   She turns and looks a moment in the glass,
Hardly aware of her departed lover;   250
Her brain allows one half-formed thought to pass:
"Well now that's done: and I'm glad it's over."
When lovely woman stoops to folly and
Paces about her room again, alone,
She smoothes her hair with automatic hand,
And puts a record on the gramophone.

   "This music crept by me upon the waters"
And along the Strand, up Queen Victoria Street.
O City city, I can sometimes hear
Beside a public bar in Lower Thames Street,   260
The pleasant whining of a mandoline
And a clatter and a chatter from within
Where fishmen lounge at noon: where the walls
Of Magnus Martyr hold
Inexplicable splendour of Ionian white and gold.

      The river sweats
   Oil and tar
   The barges drift
   With the turning tide
   Red sails   270
   Wide
   To leeward, swing on the heavy spar.
   The barges wash
   Drifting logs
   Down Greenwich reach
   Past the Isle of Dogs.
            Weialala leia
            Wallala leialala

Elizabeth and Leicester
Beating oars   280
The stern was formed
A gilded shell
Red and gold
The brisk swell
Rippled both shores
Southwest wind
Carried down stream
The peal of bells
White towers
Weialala leia   290
Wallala leialala

"Trams and dusty trees.
Highbury bore me. Richmond and Kew
Undid me. By Richmond I raised my knees
Supine on the floor of a narrow canoe."

"My feet are at Moorgate, and my heart
Under my feet. After the event
He wept. He promised 'a new start.'
I made no comment. What should I resent?"

"On Margate Sands.   300
I can connect
Nothing with nothing.
The broken fingernails of dirty hands.
My people humble people who expect
Nothing."
la la

To Carthage then I came

Burning burning burning burning
O Lord Thou pluckest me out
O Lord Thou pluckest   310

burning

IV. DEATH BY WATER

Phlebas the Phoenician, a fortnight dead,
Forgot the cry of gulls, and the deep sea swell
And the profit and loss.
              A current under sea
Picked his bones in whispers. As he rose and fell
He passed the stages of his age and youth
Entering the whirlpool.
              Gentile or Jew
O you who turn the wheel and look to windward,   320
Consider Phlebas, who was once handsome and tall as you.

V. WHAT THE THUNDER SAID

After the torchlight red on sweaty faces
After the frosty silence in the gardens
After the agony in stony places
The shouting and the crying
Prison and palace and reverberation
Of thunder of spring over distant mountains
He who was living is now dead
We who were living are now dying
With a little patience   330

    Here is no water but only rock
Rock and no water and the sandy road
The road winding above among the mountains
Which are mountains of rock without water
If there were water we should stop and drink
Amongst the rock one cannot stop or think
Sweat is dry and feet are in the sand
If there were only water amongst the rock
Dead mountain mouth of carious teeth that cannot spit
Here one can neither stand nor lie nor sit   340

There is not even silence in the mountains
But dry sterile thunder without rain
There is not even solitude in the mountains
But red sullen faces sneer and snarl
From doors of mudcracked houses
                              If there were water

    And no rock
    If there were rock
    And also water
    And water   350
    A spring
    A pool among the rock
    If there were the sound of water only
    Not the cicada
    And dry grass singing
    But sound of water over a rock
    Where the hermit-thrush sings in the pine trees
    Drip drop drip drop drop drop drop
    But there is no water

    Who is the third who walks always beside you?   360
When I count, there are only you and I together
But when I look ahead up the white road
There is always another one walking beside you
Gliding wrapt in a brown mantle, hooded
I do not know whether a man or a woman
—But who is that on the other side of you?

    What is that sound high in the air
Murmur of maternal lamentation
Who are those hooded hordes swarming
Over endless plains, stumbling in cracked earth   370
Ringed by the flat horizon only
What is the city over the mountains
Cracks and reforms and bursts in the violet air
Falling towers
Jerusalem Athens Alexandria

Vienna London
Unreal

A woman drew her long black hair out tight
And fiddled whisper music on those strings
And bats with baby faces in the violet light   380
Whistled, and beat their wings
And crawled head downward down a blackened wall
And upside down in air were towers
Tolling reminiscent bells, that kept the hours
And voices singing out of empty cisterns and exhausted
        wells.

In this decayed hole among the mountains
In the faint moonlight, the grass is singing
Over the tumbled graves, about the chapel
There is the empty chapel, only the wind's home.
It has no windows, and the door swings,   390
Dry bones can harm no one.
Only a cock stood on the rooftree
Co co rico co co rico
In a flash of lightning. Then a damp gust
Bringing rain

Ganga was sunken, and the limp leaves
Waited for rain, while the black clouds
Gathered far distant, over Himavant.
The jungle crouched, humped in silence.
Then spoke the thunder   400
DA
Datta: what have we given?
My friend, blood shaking my heart
The awful daring of a moment's surrender
Which an age of prudence can never retract
By this, and this only, we have existed
Which is not to be found in our obituaries
Or in memories draped by the beneficent spider

Or under seals broken by the lean solicitor
In our empty rooms   410
DA
Dayadhvam: I have heard the key
Turn in the door once and turn once only
We think of the key, each in his prison
Thinking of the key, each confirms a prison
Only at nightfall, aethereal rumours
Revive for a moment a broken Coriolanus
DA
Damyata: The boat responded
Gaily, to the hand expert with sail and oar   420
The sea was calm, your heart would have responded
Gaily, when invited, beating obedient
To controlling hands
                                        I sat upon the shore
Fishing, with the arid plain behind me
Shall I at least set my lands in order?
London Bridge is falling down falling down falling down
Poi s'ascose nel foco che gli affina
Quando fiam uti chelidon—O swallow swallow
Le Prince d'Aquitaine à la tour abolie   430
These fragments I have shored against my ruins
Why then Ile fit you. Hieronymo's mad againe.
Datta. Dayadhvam. Damyata.
                Shantih shantih shantih

NOTES ON "THE WASTE LAND"

Not only the title, but the plan and a good deal of the incidental
symbolism of the poem were suggested by Miss Jessie L. Weston's
book on the Grail legend: *From Ritual to Romance* (Cambridge). In-
deed, so deeply am I indebted, Miss Weston's book will elucidate
the difficulties of the poem much better than my notes can do; and
I recommend it (apart from the great interest of the book itself) to
any who think such elucidation of the poem worth the trouble. To

another work of anthropology I am indebted in general, one which has influenced our generation profoundly; I mean *The Golden Bough*; I have used especially the two volumes *Adonis, Attis, Osiris.* Anyone who is acquainted with these works will immediately recognise in the poem certain references to vegetation ceremonies.

I. THE BURIAL OF THE DEAD

Line 20. Cf. Ezekiel II, i.

23. Cf. Ecclesiastes XII, v.

31. V. Tristan und Isolde, I, verses 5–8.

42. Id. III, verse 24.

46. I am not familiar with the exact constitution of the Tarot pack of cards, from which I have obviously departed to suit my own convenience. The Hanged Man, a member of the traditional pack, fits my purpose in two ways: because he is associated in my mind with the Hanged God of Frazer, and because I associate him with the hooded figure in the passage of the disciples to Emmaus in Part V. The Phoenician Sailor and the Merchant appear later; also the "crowds of people," and Death by Water is executed in Part IV. The Man with Three Staves (an authentic member of the Tarot pack) I associate, quite arbitrarily, with the Fisher King himself.

60. Cf. Baudelaire:

"Fourmillante cité, cité pleine de rêves,

"Où le spectre en plein jour raccroche le passant."

63. Cf. Inferno III, 55–57:

"si lunga tratta

di gente, ch'io non avrei mai creduto

che morte tanta n'avesse disfatta."

64. Cf. Inferno IV, 25–27:

"Quivi, secondo che per ascoltare,

"non avea pianto, ma' che di sospiri,

"che l'aura eterna facevan tremare."

68. A phenomenon which I have often noticed.

74. Cf. the Dirge in Webster's *White Devil.*

76. V. Baudelaire, Preface to *Fleurs du Mal.*

II. A GAME OF CHESS

77. Cf. *Antony and Cleopatra*, II, ii, l. 190.

92. Laquearia. V. *Aeneid*, I, 726:

dependent lychni laquearibus aureis incensi, et noctem flammis
funalia vincunt.

98. Sylvan scene. V. Milton, *Paradise Lost,* IV, 140.

99. V. Ovid, *Metamorphoses,* VI, Philomela.

100. Cf. Part III, l. 204.

115. Cf. Part III, l. 195.

118. Cf. Webster: "Is the wind in that door still?"

126. Cf. Part I, l. 37, 48.

138. Cf. the game of chess in Middleton's *Women beware Women.*

III. THE FIRE SERMON

176. V. Spenser, *Prothalamion.*

192. Cf. *The Tempest,* I, ii.

196. Cf. Marvell, *To His Coy Mistress.*

197. Cf. Day, *Parliament of Bees:*

"When of the sudden, listening, you shall hear,

"A noise of horns and hunting, which shall bring

"Actaeon to Diana in the spring,

"Where all shall see her naked skin ..."

199. I do not know the origin of the ballad from which these lines
are taken: it was reported to me from Sydney, Australia.

202. V. Verlaine, *Parsifal.*

210. The currants were quoted at a price "carriage and insurance
free to London"; and the Bill of Lading etc. were to be handed to the
buyer upon payment of the sight draft.

218. Tiresias, although a mere spectator and not indeed a "char-
acter," is yet the most important personage in the poem, uniting all
the rest. Just as the one-eyed merchant, seller of currants, melts into
the Phoenician Sailor, and the latter is not wholly distinct from Fer-
dinand Prince of Naples, so all the women are one woman, and the
two sexes meet in Tiresias. What Tiresias *sees,* in fact, is the sub-
stance of the poem. The whole passage from Ovid is of great an-
thropological interest:

'... Cum Iunone iocos et maior vestra profecto est

Quam, quae contingit maribus,' dixisse, 'voluptas.'

Illa negat; placuit quae sit sententia docti

Quaerere Tiresiae: venus huic erat utraque nota.

Nam duo magnorum viridi coeuntia silva

Corpora serpentum baculi violaverat ictu

Deque viro factus, mirabile, femina septem
Egerat autumnos; octavo rursus eosdem
Vidit et 'est vestrae si tanta potentia plagae,'
Dixit 'ut auctoris sortem in contraria mutet,
Nunc quoque vos feriam!' percussis anguibus isdem
Forma prior rediit genetivaque venit imago.
Arbiter hic igitur sumptus de lite iocosa
Dicta Iovis firmat; gravius Saturnia iusto
Nec pro materia fertur doluisse suique
Iudicis aeterna damnavit lumina nocte,
At pater omnipotens (neque enim licet inrita cuiquam
Facta dei fecisse deo) pro lumine adempto
Scire futura dedit poenamque levavit honore.

221. This may not appear as exact as Sappho's lines, but I had in mind the "longshore" or "dory" fisherman, who returns at nightfall.

253. V. Goldsmith, the song in *The Vicar of Wakefield*.

257. V. *The Tempest*, as above.

264. The interior of St. Magnus Martyr is to my mind one of the finest among Wren's interiors. See *The Proposed Demolition of Nineteen City Churches:* (P. S. King & Son, Ltd.).

266. The Song of the (three) Thames-daughters begins here. From line 292 to 306 inclusive they speak in turn. V. *Götterdämmerung*, III, i: the Rhine-daughters.

279. V. Froude, *Elizabeth*, Vol. I, ch. iv, letter of De Quadra to Philip of Spain:

"In the afternoon we were in a barge, watching the games on the river. (The queen) was alone with Lord Robert and myself on the poop, when they began to talk nonsense, and went so far that Lord Robert at last said, as I was on the spot there was no reason why they should not be married if the queen pleased."

293. Cf. *Purgatorio*, V, 133:

"Ricorditi di me, che son la Pia;
"Siena mi fe', disfecemi Maremma."

307. V. St. Augustine's *Confessions:* "to Carthage then I came, where a cauldron of unholy loves sang all about mine ears."

308. The complete text of the Buddha's Fire Sermon (which corresponds in importance to the Sermon on the Mount) from which these words are taken, will be found translated in the late Henry Clarke Warren's *Buddhism in Translation* (Harvard Oriental Series).

Mr. Warren was one of the great pioneers of Buddhist studies in the Occident.

309. From St. Augustine's *Confessions* again. The collocation of these two representatives of eastern and western asceticism, as the culmination of this part of the poem, is not an accident.

V. WHAT THE THUNDER SAID

In the first part of Part V three themes are employed: the journey to Emmaus, the approach to the Chapel Perilous (see Miss Weston's book) and the present decay of eastern Europe.

357. This is *Turdus aonalaschkae pallasii,* the hermit-thrush which I have heard in Quebec Province. Chapman says (*Handbook of Birds of Eastern North America*) "it is most at home in secluded woodland and thickety retreats.... Its notes are not remarkable for variety or volume, but in purity and sweetness of tone and exquisite modulation they are unequalled." Its "water-dripping song" is justly celebrated.

360. The following lines were stimulated by the account of one of the Antarctic expeditions (I forget which, but I think one of Shackleton's): it was related that the party of explorers, at the extremity of their strength, had the constant delusion that there was *one more member* than could actually be counted.

367–77. Cf. Hermann Hesse, *Blick ins Chaos:* "Schon ist halb Europa, schon ist zumindest der halbe Osten Europas auf dem Wege zum Chaos, fährt betrunken im heiligem Wahn am Abgrund entlang und singt dazu, singt betrunken und hymnisch wie Dmitri Karamasoff sang. Ueber diese Lieder lacht der Bürger beleidigt, der Heilige und Seher hört sie mit Tränen."

402. "Datta, dayadhvam, damyata" (Give, sympathise, control). The fable of the meaning of the Thunder is found in the *Brihadaranyaka—Upanishad,* 5, 1. A translation is found in Deussen's *Sechzig Upanishads des Veda,* p. 489.

408. Cf. Webster, *The White Devil,* V, vi:

> "... they'll remarry
> Ere the worm pierce your winding-sheet, ere the spider
> Make a thin curtain for your epitaphs."

412. Cf. *Inferno,* XXXIII, 46:

> "ed io sentii chiavar l'uscio di sotto
> all'orribile torre."

Also F. H. Bradley, *Appearance and Reality*, p. 346.
"My external sensations are no less private to myself than are my thoughts or my feelings. In either case my experience falls within my own circle, a circle closed on the outside; and, with all its elements alike, every sphere is opaque to the others which surround it. . . . In brief, regarded as an existence which appears in a soul, the whole world for each is peculiar and private to that soul."

425. V. Weston: *From Ritual to Romance;* chapter on the Fisher King.

428. V. *Purgatorio,* XXVI, 148.

" 'Ara vos prec per aquella valor
'que vos guida al som de l'escalina,
'sovegna vos a temps de ma dolor.'
Poi s'ascose nel foco che gli affina."

429. V. *Pervigilium Veneris.* Cf. Philomela in Parts II and III.

430. V. Gerard de Nerval, Sonnet *El Desdichado.*

432. V. Kyd's *Spanish Tragedy.*

434. Shantih. Repeated as here, a formal ending to an Upanishad. "The Peace which passeth understanding" is our equivalent to this word.

THE SACRED WOOD

ESSAYS ON POETRY AND CRITICISM

For
H. W. E.
"Tacuit et Fecit"

"INTRAVIT pinacothecam senex canus, exercitati vultus et qui videretur nescio quid magnum promittere, sed cultu non proinde speciosus, et facile appareret eum ex hac nota litteratum esse, quos odisse divites solent . . . 'ego' inquit 'poeta sum et ut spero, non humillimi spiritus, si modo coronis aliquid credendum est, quas etiam ad immeritos deferre gratia solet.' "

—PETRONIUS.

"I also like to dine on becaficas."

Certain of these essays appeared, in the same or a more primitive form, in *The Times Literary Supplement, The Athenæum, Art and Letters,* and *The Egoist*. The author desires to express his obligation to the editors of these periodicals.

INTRODUCTION

To anyone who is at all capable of experiencing the pleasures of justice, it is gratifying to be able to make amends to a writer whom one has vaguely depreciated for some years. The faults and foibles of Matthew Arnold are no less evident to me now than twelve years ago, after my first admiration for him; but I hope that now, on re-reading some of his prose with more care, I can better appreciate his position. And what makes Arnold seem all the more remarkable is, that if he were our exact contemporary, he would find all his labour to perform again. A moderate number of persons have engaged in what is called "critical" writing, but no conclusion is any more solidly established than it was in 1865. In the first essay in the first *Essays in Criticism* we read that

> it has long seemed to me that the burst of creative activity in our literature, through the first quarter of this century, had about it in fact something premature; and that from this cause its productions are doomed, most of them, in spite of the sanguine hopes which accompanied and do still accompany them, to prove hardly more lasting than the productions of far less splendid epochs. And this prematureness comes from its having proceeded without having its proper data, without sufficient material to work with. In other words, the English poetry of the first quarter of this century, with plenty of energy, plenty of creative force, did not know enough. This makes Byron so empty of mat-

ter, Shelley so incoherent, Wordsworth even, profound as he is, yet so wanting in completeness and variety.

This judgment of the Romantic Generation has not, so far as I know, ever been successfully controverted; and it has not, so far as I know, ever made very much impression on popular opinion. Once a poet is accepted, his reputation is seldom disturbed, for better or worse. So little impression has Arnold's opinion made, that his statement will probably be as true of the first quarter of the twentieth century as it was of the nineteenth. A few sentences later, Arnold articulates the nature of the malady:

> In the Greece of Pindar and Sophocles, in the England of Shakespeare, the poet lived in a current of ideas in the highest degree animating and nourishing to the creative power; society was, in the fullest measure, permeated by fresh thought, intelligent and alive; and this state of things is the true basis for the creative power's exercise, in this it finds its data, its materials, truly ready for its hand; all the books and reading in the world are only valuable as they are helps to this.

At this point Arnold is indicating the centre of interest and activity of the critical intelligence; and it is at this perception, we may almost say, that Arnold's critical activity stopped. In a society in which the arts were seriously studied, in which the art of writing was respected, Arnold might have become a critic. How astonishing it would be, if a man like Arnold had concerned himself with the art of the novel, had compared Thackeray with Flaubert, had analysed the work of Dickens, had shown his contemporaries exactly why the author of *Amos Barton* is a more *serious* writer than Dickens, and why the author of *La Chartreuse de Parme* is more serious than either? In *Culture and Anarchy*, in *Literature and Dogma*, Arnold was not occupied so much in establishing a criticism as in attacking the uncritical. The difference is that while in constructive work something can be done, destructive work must incessantly be repeated; and furthermore Arnold, in his destruction, went for game outside of the literary preserve altogether, much of it political game untouched and inviolable by ideas. This activity of Arnold's we must regret; it might perhaps have been carried on as effectively, if not quite so neatly, by some disciple (had there been one) in an editorial position on a newspaper. Arnold is not to be blamed: he wasted his strength, as men of superior ability sometimes do, because he saw something to be done and no one else to do it. The temptation, to any man who is interested in ideas and primarily in literature, to put literature into the corner until he has cleaned up the whole country first, is almost irresistible. Some persons, like Mr. Wells and Mr. Chesterton, have succeeded so well in this latter profession of setting the house in order, and have attracted so much more attention than Arnold, that we must conclude that it is indeed their proper rôle, and that they have done well for themselves in laying literature aside.

Not only is the critic tempted outside of criticism. The criticism proper betrays such poverty of ideas and such atrophy of sensibility that men who ought to preserve their critical ability for the improvement of their own creative work are tempted into criticism. I do not intend from this the usually silly inference that the "creative" gift is "higher" than the critical. When one creative mind is better than another, the reason often is that the better is the more critical. But the great bulk of the work of criticism could be done by minds of the second order, and it is just these minds of the second order that are difficult to find. They are necessary for the rapid circulation of ideas. The periodical press—the ideal literary periodical—is an instrument of transport; and the literary periodical press is dependent upon the existence of a sufficient number of second-order (I do not say "second-rate," the word is too derogatory) minds to supply its material. These minds are necessary for that "current of ideas," that "society permeated by fresh thought," of which Arnold speaks.

It is a perpetual heresy of English culture to believe that

only the first-order mind, the Genius, the Great Man, matters; that he is solitary, and produced best in the least favourable environment, perhaps the Public School; and that it is most likely a sign of inferiority that Paris can show so many minds of the second order. If too much bad verse is published in London, it does not occur to us to raise our standards, to do anything to educate the poetasters; the remedy is, Kill them off. I quote from Mr. Edmund Gosse:[1]

> Unless something is done to stem this flood of poetastry the art of verse will become not merely superfluous, but ridiculous. Poetry is not a formula which a thousand flappers and hobbledehoys ought to be able to master in a week without any training, and the mere fact that it seems to be now practised with such universal ease is enough to prove that something has gone amiss with our standards. . . . This is all wrong, and will lead us down into the abyss like so many Gadarene swine unless we resist it.

We quite agree that poetry is not a formula. But what does Mr. Gosse propose to do about it? If Mr. Gosse had found himself in the flood of poetastry in the reign of Elizabeth, what would he have done about it? would he have stemmed it? What exactly is this abyss? and if something "has gone amiss with our standards," is it wholly the fault of the younger generation that it is aware of no authority that it must respect? It is part of the business of the critic to preserve tradition—where a good tradition exists. It is part of his business to see literature steadily and to see it whole; and this is eminently to see it *not* as consecrated by time, but to see it beyond time; to see the best work of our time and the best work of twenty-five hundred years ago with the same eyes.[2] It is part of his business to help the poetaster to understand his own limitations. The poetaster who understands his own limitations will be

---

[1] *Sunday Times,* May 30, 1920.

[2] Arnold, it must be admitted, gives us often the impression of seeing the masters, whom he quotes, as canonical literature, rather than as masters.

one of our useful second-order minds; a good minor poet (something which is very rare) or another good critic. As for the first-order minds, when they happen, they will be none the worse off for a "current of ideas"; the solitude with which they will always and everywhere be invested is a very different thing from isolation, or a monarchy of death.

NOTE.—I may commend as a model to critics who desire to correct some of the poetical vagaries of the present age, the following passage from a writer who cannot be accused of flaccid leniency, and the justice of whose criticism must be acknowledged even by those who feel a strong partiality toward the school of poets criticized:—

> Yet great labour, directed by great abilities, is never wholly lost; if they frequently threw away their wit upon false conceits, they likewise sometimes struck out unexpected truth: if their conceits were far-fetched, they were often worth the carriage. To write on their plan, it was at least necessary to read and think. No man could be born a metaphysical poet, nor assume the dignity of a writer, by descriptions copied from descriptions, by imitations borrowed from imitations, by traditional imagery, and hereditary similes, by readiness of rhyme, and volubility of syllables.
>
> In perusing the works of this race of authors, the mind is exercised either by recollection or inquiry: something already learned is to be retrieved, or something new is to be examined. If their greatness seldom elevates, their acuteness often surprises; if the imagination is not always gratified, at least the powers of reflection and comparison are employed; and in the mass of materials which ingenious absurdity has thrown together, genuine wit and useful knowledge may be sometimes found buried perhaps in grossness of expression, but useful to those who know their value; and such as, when they are expanded to perspicuity, and polished to elegance, may give lustre to works which have more propriety though less copiousness of sentiment.—JOHNSON, *Life of Cowley.*

THE PERFECT CRITIC

I

"Eriger en lois ses impressions personnelles, c'est le grand effort d'un homme s'il est sincère."

—LETTRES À L'AMAZONE

Coleridge was perhaps the greatest of English critics, and in a sense the last. After Coleridge we have Matthew Arnold; but Arnold—I think it will be conceded—was rather a propagandist for criticism than a critic, a popularizer rather than a creator of ideas. So long as this island remains an island (and we are no nearer the Continent than were Arnold's contemporaries) the work of Arnold will be important; it is still a bridge across the Channel, and it will always have been good sense. Since Arnold's attempt to correct his countrymen, English criticism has followed two directions. When a distinguished critic observed recently, in a newspaper article, that "poetry is the most highly organized form of intellectual activity," we were conscious that we were reading neither Coleridge nor Arnold. Not only have the words "organized" and "activity," occurring together in this phrase, that familiar vague suggestion of the scientific vocabulary which is characteristic of modern writing, but one asked questions which Coleridge and Arnold would not have permitted one to ask. How is it, for instance, that poetry is more "highly organized" than astronomy, physics, or pure mathematics, which we imagine to be, in relation to the scientist who practises them, "intellectual activity" of a pretty highly organized type? "Mere strings of words," our critic continues with felicity and truth, "flung like dabs of paint across a blank canvas, may awaken surprise . . . but have no significance whatever in the history of literature." The phrases by which Arnold is best known may be inadequate, they may assemble more doubts than they dispel, but they usually have some meaning. And if a phrase like "the most highly organized form of intellectual activity" is the highest organization of thought of which contemporary criticism, in a distinguished representative, is capable, then, we conclude, modern criticism is degenerate.

The verbal disease above noticed may be reserved for diagnosis by and by. It is not a disease from which Mr. Arthur Symons (for the quotation was, of course, not from Mr. Symons) notably suffers. Mr. Symons represents the other tendency; he is a representative of what is always called "æsthetic criticism" or "impressionistic criticism." And it is this form of criticism which I propose to examine at once. Mr. Symons, the critical successor of Pater, and partly of Swinburne (I fancy that the phrase "sick or sorry" is the common property of all three), *is* the "impressionistic critic." He, if anyone, would be said to expose a sensitive and cultivated mind—cultivated, that is, by the accumulation of a considerable variety of impressions from all the arts and several languages—before an "object"; and his criticism, if anyone's, would be said to exhibit to us, like the plate, the faithful record of the impressions, more numerous or more refined than our own. A record, we observe, which is also an interpretation, a translation; for it must itself impose impressions upon us, and these impressions are as much created as transmitted by the criticism. I do not say at once that this is Mr. Symons; but it is the "impressionistic" critic, and the impressionistic critic is supposed to be Mr. Symons.

At hand is a volume which we may test.[1] Ten of these thir-teen essays deal with single plays of Shakespeare, and it is therefore fair to take one of these ten as a specimen of the book:

> *Antony and Cleopatra* is the most wonderful, I think, of all Shake-speare's plays . . .

and Mr. Symons reflects that Cleopatra is the most wonderful of all women:

> The queen who ends the dynasty of the Ptolemies has been the star of poets, a malign star shedding baleful light, from Horace and Propertius down to Victor Hugo; and it is not to poets only . . .

What, we ask, is this for? as a page on Cleopatra, and on her possible origin in the dark lady of the Sonnets, unfolds itself. And we find, gradually, that this is not an essay on a work of art or a work of intellect; but that Mr. Symons is living through the play as one might live it through in the theatre; recounting, commenting:

> In her last days Cleopatra touches a certain elevation . . . she would die a thousand times, rather than live to be a mockery and a scorn in men's mouths . . . she is a woman to the last . . . so she dies . . . the play ends with a touch of grave pity . . .

Presented in this rather unfair way, torn apart like the leaves of an artichoke, the impressions of Mr. Symons come to resemble a common type of popular literary lecture, in which the stories of plays or novels are retold, the motives of the characters set forth, and the work of art therefore made easier for the beginner. But this is not Mr. Symons' reason for writing. The reason why we find a similarity between his

[1] *Studies in Elizabethan Drama.* By Arthur Symons.

essay and this form of education is that *Antony and Cleopatra* is a play with which we are pretty well acquainted, and of which we have, therefore, our own impressions. We can please ourselves with our own impressions of the characters and their emotions; and we do not find the impressions of another person, however sensitive, very significant. But if we can recall the time when we were ignorant of the French symbolists, and met with *The Symbolist Movement in Literature,* we remember that book as an introduction to wholly new feelings, as a revelation. After we have read Verlaine and Laforgue and Rimbaud and return to Mr. Symons' book, we may find that our own impressions dissent from his. The book has not, perhaps, a permanent value for the one reader, but it has led to results of permanent importance for him.

The question is not whether Mr. Symons' impressions are "true" or "false." So far as you can isolate the "impression," the pure feeling, it is, of course, neither true nor false. The point is that you never rest at the pure feeling; you react in one of two ways, or, as I believe Mr. Symons does, in a mixture of the two ways. The moment you try to put the impressions into words, you either begin to analyse and construct, to "ériger en lois," or you begin to create something else. It is significant that Swinburne, by whose poetry Mr. Symons may at one time have been influenced, is one man in his poetry and a different man in his criticism; to this extent and in this respect only, that he is satisfying a different impulse; he is criticizing, expounding, arranging. You may say this is not the criticism of a critic, that it is emotional, not intellectual— though of this there are two opinions, but it is in the direction of analysis and construction, a beginning to "ériger en lois," and not in the direction of creation. So I infer that Swinburne found an adequate outlet for the creative impulse in his poetry; and none of it was forced back and out through his critical prose. The style of the latter is essentially a prose style; and Mr. Symons' prose is much more like Swinburne's poetry than it is like his prose. I imagine—though here one's thought is moving in almost complete darkness—that Mr. Symons is far more disturbed, far more profoundly affected, by his reading than was Swinburne, who responded rather by a violent and immediate and comprehensive burst of admiration which may have left him internally unchanged. The disturbance in Mr. Symons is almost, but not quite, to the point of creating; the reading sometimes fecundates his emotions to produce something new which is not criticism, but is not the expulsion, the ejection, the birth of creativeness.

The type is not uncommon, although Mr. Symons is far superior to most of the type. Some writers are essentially of the type that reacts in excess of the stimulus, making something new out of the impressions, but suffer from a defect of vitality or an obscure obstruction which prevents nature from taking its course. Their sensibility alters the object, but never transforms it. Their reaction is that of the ordinary emotional person developed to an exceptional degree. For this ordinary emotional person, experiencing a work of art, has a mixed critical and creative reaction. It is made up of comment and opinion, and also new emotions which are vaguely applied to his own life. The sentimental person, in whom a work of art arouses all sorts of emotions which have nothing to do with that work of art whatever, but are accidents of personal association, is an incomplete artist. For in an artist these suggestions made by a work of art, which are purely personal, become fused with a multitude of other suggestions from multitudinous experience, and result in the production of a new object which is no longer purely personal, because it is a work of art itself.

It would be rash to speculate, and is perhaps impossible to determine, what is unfulfilled in Mr. Symons' charming verse that overflows into his critical prose. Certainly we may say that in Swinburne's verse the circuit of impression and expression is complete; and Swinburne was therefore able, in his criticism, to be more a critic than Mr. Symons. This gives us an intimation why the artist is—each within his own limitations—oftenest to be depended upon as a critic; his criticism will be criticism, and not the satisfaction of a suppressed creative wish—which, in most other persons, is apt to interfere fatally.

Before considering what the proper critical reaction of artistic sensibility is, how far criticism is "feeling" and how far "thought," and what sort of "thought" is permitted, it may be instructive to prod a little into that other temperament, so different from Mr. Symons', which issues in generalities such as that quoted near the beginning of this article.

II

"L'écrivain de style abstrait est presque toujours un sentimental, du moins un sensitif. L'écrivain artiste n'est presque jamais un sentimental, et très rarement un sensitif."

—LE PROBLÈME DU STYLE

The statement already quoted, that "poetry is the most highly organized form of intellectual activity," may be taken as a specimen of the abstract style in criticism. The confused distinction which exists in most heads between "abstract" and "concrete" is due not so much to a manifest fact of the existence of two types of mind, an abstract and a concrete, as to the existence of another type of mind, the verbal, or philosophic. I, of course, do not imply any general condemnation of philosophy; I am, for the moment, using the word "philosophic" to cover the unscientific ingredients of philosophy; to cover, in fact, the greater part of the philosophic output of the last hundred years. There are two ways in which a word may be "abstract." It may have (the word "activity," for example) a meaning which cannot be grasped by appeal to any of the senses; its apprehension may require a deliberate suppression of analogies of visual or muscular experience, which is none the less an effort of imagination. "Activity" will mean for the trained scientist, if he employ the term, either nothing at all or something still more exact than anything it suggests to us.

If we are allowed to accept certain remarks of Pascal and Mr. Bertrand Russell about mathematics, we believe that the mathematician deals with objects—if he will permit us to call them objects—which directly affect his sensibility. And during a good part of history the philosopher endeavoured to deal with objects which he believed to be of the same exactness as the mathematician's. Finally Hegel arrived, and if not perhaps the first, he was certainly the most prodigious exponent of emotional systematization, dealing with his emotions as if they were definite objects which had aroused those emotions. His followers have as a rule taken for granted that words have definite meanings, overlooking the tendency of words to become indefinite emotions. (No one who had not witnessed the event could imagine the conviction in the tone of Professor Eucken as he pounded the table and exclaimed *Was ist Geist? Geist ist . . .*) If verbalism were confined to professional philosophers, no harm would be done. But their corruption has extended very far. Compare a mediæval theologian or mystic, compare a seventeenth-century preacher, with any "liberal" sermon since Schleiermacher, and you will observe that words have changed their meanings. What they have lost is definite, and what they have gained is indefinite.

The vast accumulations of knowledge—or at least of information—deposited by the nineteenth century have been responsible for an equally vast ignorance. When there is so much to be known, when there are so many fields of knowledge in which the same words are used with different meanings, when every one knows a little about a great many things, it becomes increasingly difficult for anyone to know whether he knows what he is talking about or not. And when we do not know, or when we do not know enough, we tend always to substitute emotions for thoughts. The sentence so frequently quoted in this essay will serve for an example of this process as well as any, and may be profitably contrasted with the opening phrases of the *Posterior Analytics*. Not only all knowledge, but all feeling, is in perception. The inventor of poetry as the most highly organized form of intellectual activity was not engaged in perceiving when he composed this definition; he had nothing to be aware of except his own emotion about "poetry." He was, in fact, absorbed in a very different "activity" not only from that of Mr. Symons, but from that of Aristotle.

Aristotle is a person who has suffered from the adherence of persons who must be regarded less as his disciples than as his sectaries. One must be firmly distrustful of accepting Aristotle in a canonical spirit; this is to lose the whole living force of him. He was primarily a man of not only remarkable but universal intelligence; and universal intelligence means that he could apply his intelligence to anything. The ordinary intelligence is good only for certain classes of objects; a brilliant man of science, if he is interested in poetry at all, may conceive grotesque judgments: like one poet because he reminds him of himself, or another because he expresses emotions which he admires; he may use art, in fact, as the outlet for the egotism which is suppressed in his own speciality. But Aristotle had none of these impure desires to satisfy; in whatever sphere of interest, he looked solely and steadfastly at the object; in his short and broken treatise he provides an eternal example—not of laws, or even of method, for there is no method except to be very intelligent, but of intelligence itself swiftly operating the analysis of sensation to the point of principle and definition.

It is far less Aristotle than Horace who has been the model for criticism up to the nineteenth century. A precept, such as Horace or Boileau gives us, is merely an unfinished analysis. It appears as a law, a rule, because it does not appear in its most general form; it is empirical. When we understand necessity, as Spinoza knew, we are free because we assent. The dogmatic critic, who lays down a rule, who affirms a value, has left his labour incomplete. Such statements may often be justifiable as a saving of time; but in matters of great importance the critic must not coerce, and he must not make judgments of worse and better. He must simply elucidate: the reader will form the correct judgment for himself.

And again, the purely "technical" critic—the critic, that is, who writes to expound some novelty or impart some lesson to practitioners of an art—can be called a critic only in a narrow sense. He may be analysing perceptions and the means for arousing perceptions, but his aim is limited and is not the disinterested exercise of intelligence. The narrowness of the aim makes easier the detection of the merit or feebleness of the work; even of these writers there are very few—so that their "criticism" is of great importance within its limits. So much suffices for Campion. Dryden is far more disinterested; he displays much free intelligence; and yet even Dryden—or any *literary* critic of the seventeenth century—is not quite a free mind, compared, for instance, with such a mind as Rochefoucauld's. There is always a tendency to legislate rather than to inquire, to revise accepted laws, even to overturn, but to reconstruct out of the same material. And the free intelligence is that which is wholly devoted to inquiry.

Coleridge, again, whose natural abilities, and some of whose performances, are probably more remarkable than those of any other modern critic, cannot be estimated as an intelligence completely free. The nature of the restraint in his case is quite different from that which limited the seventeenth-century critics, and is much more personal. Coleridge's metaphysical interest was quite genuine, and was, like most metaphysical interest, an affair of his emotions. But a literary critic should have no emotions except those immediately provoked by a work of art—and these (as I have already hinted) are, when valid, perhaps not to be called emotions at all. Coleridge is apt to take leave of the data of criticism, and arouse the suspicion that he has been diverted into a metaphysical hare-and-hounds. His end does not always appear to be the return to the work of art with improved perception and intensified, because more conscious, enjoyment; his centre of interest changes, his feelings are impure. In the derogatory sense he is more "philosophic" than Aristotle. For everything that Aristotle says illuminates the literature which is the occasion for saying it; but Coleridge only now and then. It is one more instance of the pernicious effect of emotion.

Aristotle had what is called the scientific mind—a mind which, as it is rarely found among scientists except in fragments, might better be called the intelligent mind. For there is no other intelligence than this, and so far as artists and men of letters are intelligent (we may doubt whether the level of intelligence among men of letters is as high as among men of science) their intelligence is of this kind. Sainte-Beuve was a physiologist by training; but it is probable that his mind, like that of the ordinary scientific specialist, was limited in its interest, and that this was not, primarily, an interest in art. If he was a critic, there is no doubt that he was a very good one; but we may conclude that he earned some other name. Of all modern critics, perhaps Remy de Gourmont had most of the general intelligence of Aristotle. An amateur, though an excessively able amateur, in physiology, he combined to a remarkable degree sensitiveness, erudition, sense of fact and sense of history, and generalizing power.

We assume the gift of a superior sensibility. And for sensibility wide and profound reading does not mean merely a more extended pasture. There is not merely an increase of understanding, leaving the original acute impression unchanged. The new impressions modify the impressions received from the objects already known. An impression needs to be constantly refreshed by new impressions in order that it may persist at all; it needs to take its place in a system of impressions. And this system tends to become articulate in a generalized statement of literary beauty.

There are, for instance, many scattered lines and tercets in the *Divine Comedy* which are capable of transporting even a quite uninitiated reader, just sufficiently acquainted with the roots of the language to decipher the meaning, to an impression of overpowering beauty. This impression may be so deep that no subsequent study and understanding will intensify it. But at this point the impression is emotional; the reader in the ignorance which we postulate is unable to distinguish the poetry from an emotional state aroused in himself by the poetry, a state which may be merely an indulgence of his own emotions. The poetry may be an accidental stimulus. The end of the enjoyment of poetry is a pure contemplation from which all the accidents of personal emotion are removed; thus we aim to see the object as it really is and find a meaning for the words of Arnold. And without a labour which is largely a labour of the intelligence, we are unable to attain that stage of vision *amor intellectualis Dei*.

Such considerations, cast in this general form, may appear commonplaces. But I believe that it is always opportune to call attention to the torpid superstition that appreciation is one thing, and "intellectual" criticism something else. Appreciation in popular psychology is one faculty, and criticism another, an arid cleverness building theoretical scaffolds upon one's own perceptions or those of others. On the contrary, the true generalization is not something superposed upon an accumulation of perceptions; the perceptions do not, in a really appreciative mind, accumulate as a mass, but form themselves as a structure; and criticism is the statement in language of this structure; it is a development of sensibility. The bad criticism, on the other hand, is that which is nothing but an expression of emotion. And emotional people—such as stockbrokers, politicians, men of science—and a few people who pride themselves on being unemotional—detest or applaud great writers such as Spinoza or Stendhal because of their "frigidity."

The writer of the present essay once committed himself to the statement that "The poetic critic is criticizing poetry in order to create poetry." He is now inclined to believe that the "historical" and the "philosophical" critics had better be called historians and philosophers quite simply. As for the rest, there are merely various degrees of intelligence. It is fatuous to say that criticism is for the sake of "creation" or creation for the sake of criticism. It is also fatuous to assume that there are ages of criticism and ages of creativeness, as if by plunging ourselves into intellectual darkness we were in better hope of finding spiritual light. The two directions of sensibility are complementary; and as sensibility is rare, unpopular, and desirable, it is to be expected that the critic and the creative artist should frequently be the same person.

IMPERFECT CRITICS

SWINBURNE AS CRITIC

Three conclusions at least issue from the perusal of Swinburne's critical essays: Swinburne had mastered his material, was more inward with the Tudor-Stuart dramatists than any man of pure letters before or since; he is a more reliable guide to them than Hazlitt, Coleridge, or Lamb; and his perception of relative values is almost always correct. Against these merits we may oppose two objections: the style is the prose style of Swinburne, and the content is not, in an exact sense, criticism. The faults of style are, of course, personal; the tumultuous outcry of adjectives, the headstrong rush of undisciplined sentences, are the index to the impatience and perhaps laziness of a disorderly mind. But the style has one positive merit: it allows us to know that Swinburne was writing not to establish a critical reputation, not to instruct a docile public, but as a poet his notes upon poets whom he admired. And whatever our opinion of Swinburne's verse, the notes upon poets by a poet of Swinburne's dimensions must be read with attention and respect.

In saying that Swinburne's essays have the value of notes of an important poet upon important poets, we must place a check upon our expectancy. He read everything, and he read with the single interest in finding literature. The critics of the romantic period were pioneers, and exhibit the fallibility of discoverers. The selections of Lamb are a successful effort of good taste, but anyone who has referred to them after a thorough reading of any of the poets included must have found that some of the best passages—which must literally have stared Lamb in the face—are omitted, while sometimes others of less value are included. Hazlitt, who committed himself to the judgment that the *Maid's Tragedy* is one of the poorest of Beaumont and Fletcher's plays, has no connected message to deliver. Coleridge's remarks—too few and scattered—have permanent truth; but on some of the greatest names he passes no remark, and of some of the best plays was perhaps ignorant or ill-informed. But compared with Swinburne, Coleridge writes much more as a poet might be expected to write about poets. Of Massinger's verse Swinburne says:

> It is more serviceable, more businesslike, more eloquently practical, and more rhetorically effusive—but never effusive beyond the bounds of effective rhetoric—than the style of any Shakespearean or of any Jonsonian dramatist.

It is impossible to tell whether Webster would have found the style of Massinger more "serviceable" than his own for the last act of the *White Devil,* and indeed difficult to decide what "serviceable" here means; but it is quite clear what Coleridge means when he says that Massinger's style

> is much more easily constructed [than Shakespeare's], and may be more successfully adopted by writers in the present day.

Coleridge is writing as a professional with his eye on the technique. I do not know from what writing of Coleridge Swinburne draws the assertion that "Massinger often deals in exaggerated passion," but in the essay from which Swinburne quotes elsewhere Coleridge merely speaks of the "unnaturally irrational passions," a phrase much more defensible.

Upon the whole, the two poets are in harmony upon the subject of Massinger; and although Coleridge has said more in five pages, and said it more clearly, than Swinburne in thirtynine, the essay of Swinburne is by no means otiose: it is more stimulating than Coleridge's, and the stimulation is never misleading. With all his superlatives, his judgment, if carefully scrutinized, appears temperate and just.

With all his justness of judgment, however, Swinburne is an appreciator and not a critic. In the whole range of literature covered, Swinburne makes hardly more than two judgments which can be reversed or even questioned: one, that Lyly is insignificant as a dramatist, and the other, that Shirley was probably unaffected by Webster. The *Cardinal* is not a cast of the *Duchess of Malfi,* certainly; but when Shirley wrote

> the mist is risen, and there's none
> To steer my wandering bark. *(Dies.)*

he was probably affected by

> My soul, like to a ship in a black storm,
> Is driven, I know not whither.

Swinburne's judgment is generally sound, his taste sensitive and discriminating. And we cannot say that his thinking is faulty or perverse—up to the point at which it is thinking. But Swinburne stops thinking just at the moment when we are most zealous to go on. And this arrest, while it does not vitiate his work, makes it an introduction rather than a statement.

We are aware, after the *Contemporaries of Shakespeare* and the *Age of Shakespeare* and the books on Shakespeare and Jonson, that there is something unsatisfactory in the way in which Swinburne was interested in these people; we suspect that his interest was never articulately formulated in his mind or consciously directed to any purpose. He makes his way, or loses it, between two paths of definite direction. He might as a poet have concentrated his attention upon the technical problems solved or tackled by these men; he might have traced for us the development of blank verse from Sackville to the mature Shakespeare, and its degeneration from Shakespeare to Milton. Or he might have studied through the literature to the mind of that century; he might, by dissection and analysis, have helped us to some insight into the feeling and thought which we seem to have left so far away. In either case, you would have had at least the excitement of following the movements of an important mind groping towards important conclusions. As it is, there are to be no conclusions, except that Elizabethan literature is very great, and that you can have pleasure and even ecstasy from it, because a sensitive poetic talent has had the experience. One is in risk of becoming fatigued by a hubbub that does not march; the drum is beaten, but the procession does not advance.

If, for example, Swinburne's interest was in poetry, why devote an essay to Brome? "The opening scene of the *Sparagus Garden*," says Swinburne, "is as happily humorous and as vividly natural as that of any more famous comedy." The scene is both humorous and natural. Brome deserves to be more read than he is, and first of all to be more accessible than he is. But Swinburne ought to suggest or imply (I do not say impose) a reason for reading the *Sparagus Garden* or the *Antipodes*, more sufficient than any he has provided. No doubt such reason could be found.

When it is a matter of pronouncing judgment between two poets, Swinburne is almost unerring. He is certainly right in putting Webster above Tourneur, Tourneur above Ford, and Ford above Shirley. He weighs accurately the good and evil in Fletcher: he perceives the essential theatricality, but his comparison of the *Faithful Shepherdess* with *Comus* is a judgment no word of which can be improved upon:

> The difference between this poem [*i.e.* the *Faithful Shepherdess*] and Milton's exquisitely imitative *Comus* is the difference be-

tween a rose with a leaf or two faded or falling, but still fragrant and radiant, and the faultless but scentless reproduction of a rose in academic wax for the admiration and imitation of such craftsmen as must confine their ambition to the laurels of a college or the plaudits of a school.

In the longest and most important essay in the *Contemporaries of Shakespeare,* the essay on Chapman, there are many such sentences of sound judgment forcibly expressed. The essay is the best we have on that great poet. It communicates the sense of dignity and mass which we receive from Chapman. But it also illustrates Swinburne's infirmities. Swinburne was not tormented by the restless desire to penetrate to the heart and marrow of a poet, any more than he was tormented by the desire to render the finest shades of difference and resemblance between several poets. Chapman is a difficult author, as Swinburne says; he is far more difficult than Jonson, to whom he bears only a superficial likeness. He is difficult beyond his obscurity. He is difficult partly through his possession of a quality comparatively deficient in Jonson, but which was nevertheless a quality of the age. It is strange that Swinburne should have hinted at a similarity to Jonson and not mentioned a far more striking affinity of Chapman's—that is, Donne. The man who wrote

> Guise, O my lord, how shall I cast from me
> The bands and coverts hindering me from thee?
> The garment or the cover of the mind
> The humane soul is; of the soul, the spirit
> The proper robe is; of the spirit, the blood;
> And of the blood, the body is the shroud

and

> Nothing is made of nought, of all things made,
> Their abstract being a dream but of a shade,

is unquestionably kin to Donne. The quality in question is not peculiar to Donne and Chapman. In common with the greatest—Marlowe, Webster, Tourneur, and Shakespeare—they had a quality of sensuous thought, or of thinking through the senses, or of the senses thinking, of which the exact formula remains to be defined. If you look for it in Shelley or Beddoes, both of whom in very different ways recaptured something of the Elizabethan inspiration, you will not find it, though you may find other qualities instead. There is a trace of it only in Keats, and, derived from a different source, in Rossetti. You will not find it in the *Duke of Gandia*. Swinburne's essay would have been all the better if he had applied himself to the solution of problems like this.

He did not apply himself to this sort of problem because this was not the sort of problem that interested him. The author of Swinburne's critical essays is also the author of Swinburne's verse: if you hold the opinion that Swinburne was a very great poet, you can hardly deny him the title of a great critic. There is the same curious mixture of qualities to produce Swinburne's own effect, resulting in the same blur, which only the vigour of the colours fixes. His great merit as a critic is really one which, like many signal virtues, can be stated so simply as to appear flat. It is that he was sufficiently interested in his subject-matter and knew quite enough about it; and this is a rare combination in English criticism. Our critics are often interested in extracting something from their subject which is not fairly in it. And it is because this elementary virtue is so rare that Swinburne must take a very respectable place as a critic. Critics are often interested—but not quite in the nominal subject, often in something a little beside the point; they are often learned—but not quite to the point either. (Swinburne knew some of the plays almost by heart.) Can this particular virtue at which we have glanced be attributed to Walter Pater? or to Professor Bradley? or to Swinburne's editor?

A ROMANTIC ARISTOCRAT

It is impossible to overlook the merits of scholarship and criticism exhibited by George Wyndham's posthumous book, and it is impossible to deal with the book purely on its merits of scholarship and criticism. To attempt to do so would in the first place be unfair, as the book is a posthumous work, and posthumous books demand some personal attention to their writers. This book is a collection of essays and addresses, arranged in their present order by Mr. Whibley; they were intended by their author to be remodelled into a volume on "romantic literature"; they move from an ingenious search for the date of the beginning of Romanticism, through the French and English Renaissance, to Sir Walter Scott. In the second place, these essays represent the literary work of a man who gained his chief distinction in political life. In the third place, this man stands for a type, an English type. The type is interesting and will probably become extinct. It is natural, therefore, that our primary interest in the essays should be an interest in George Wyndham.

Mr. Charles Whibley, in an introduction the tone of which is well suited to the matter, has several sentences which throw light on Wyndham's personality. What issues with surprising clearness from Mr. Whibley's sketch is the unity of Wyndham's mind, the identity of his mind as it engaged in apparently unrelated occupations. Wyndham left Eton for the army; in barracks he "taught himself Italian, and filled his leisure with the reading of history and poetry." After this Coldstream culture there was a campaign in Egypt; later, service in South Africa accompanied by a copy of Virgil. There was a career in the Commons, a conspicuous career as Irish Secretary. Finally, there was a career as a landowner—2400 acres. And throughout these careers George Wyndham went on not only accumulating books but reading them, and occasionally writing about them. He was a man of character, a man of energy. Mr. Whibley is quite credible when he says:

> Literature was for him no parergon, no mere way of escape from politics. If he was an amateur in feeling, he was a craftsman in execution;

and, more significantly,

> With the same zest that he read and discoursed upon *A Winter's Tale* or *Troilus and Cressida*, he rode to hounds, or threw himself with a kind of fury into a "point to point," or made a speech at the hustings, or sat late in the night talking with a friend.

From these and other sentences we chart the mind of George Wyndham, and the key to its topography is the fact that his literature and his politics and his country life are one and the same thing. They are not in separate compartments, they are one career. Together they made up his world: literature, politics, riding to hounds. In the real world these things have nothing to do with each other. But we cannot believe that George Wyndham lived in the real world. And this is implied in Mr. Whibley's remark that:

> George Wyndham was by character and training a romantic. He looked with wonder upon the world as upon a fairyland.

Here is the manifestation of type.

There must probably be conceded to history a few "many-sided" men. Perhaps Leonardo da Vinci was such. George Wyndham was not a man on the scale of Leonardo, and his writings give a very different effect from Leonardo's notebooks. Leonardo turned to art or science, and each was what it was and not another thing. But Leonardo was Leonardo: he had no father to speak of, he was hardly a citizen, and he had no stake in the community. He lived in no fairyland, but his

mind went out and became a part of things. George Wynd-
ham was Gentry. He was chivalrous, the world was an adven-
ture of himself. It is characteristic that on embarking as a
subaltern for Egypt he wrote enthusiastically:

> I do not suppose that any expedition since the days of Roman
> governors of provinces has started with such magnificence; we
> might have been Antony going to Egypt in a purple-sailed galley.

This is precisely the spirit which animates his appreciation
of the Elizabethans and of Walter Scott; which guides him
toward Hakluyt and North. Wyndham was enthusiastic, he
was a Romantic, he was an Imperialist, and he was quite natu-
rally a literary pupil of W. E. Henley. Wyndham was a scholar,
but his scholarship is incidental; he was a good critic, within
the range allowed him by his enthusiasms; but it is neither as
Scholar nor as Critic that we can criticize him. We can criti-
cize his writings only as the expression of this peculiar En-
glish type, the aristocrat, the Imperialist, the Romantic, riding
to hounds across his prose, looking with wonder upon the
world as upon a fairyland.

Because he belongs to this type, Wyndham wrote enthusi-
astically and well about North's Plutarch. The romance of
the ancient world becomes more romantic in the idiomatic
prose of North; the heroes are not merely Greek and Roman
heroes, but Elizabethan heroes as well; the romantic fusion
allured Wyndham. The charms of North could not be ex-
pounded more delightfully, more seductively, with more
gusto, than they are in Wyndham's essay. He appreciates the
battles, the torchlight, the "dead sound" of drums, the white,
worn face of Cicero in his flight peering from his litter; he ap-
preciates the sharp brusque phrase of North: "he roundly
trussed them up and hung them by their necks." And Wynd-
ham is learned. Here, as in his essays on the Pléiade and
Shakespeare, the man has read everything, with a labour that
only whets his enjoyment of the best. There are two defects: a

lack of balance and a lack of critical profundity. The lack of balance peeps through Wyndham's condemnation of an obviously inferior translation of Plutarch: "He dedicated the superfluity of his leisure to enjoyment, and used his Lamia," says the bad translator. North: "he took pleasure of Lamia." Wyndham makes a set upon the bad translator. But he forgets that "dedicated the superfluity of his leisure" is such a phrase as Gibbon would have warmed to life and wit, and that a history, in the modern sense, could not be written in the style of North. Wyndham forgets, in short, that it is not, in the end, periods and traditions but individual men who write great prose. For Wyndham is himself a period and a tradition.

The lack of balance is to be suspected elsewhere. Wyndham *likes* the best, but he likes a good deal. There is no conclusive evidence that he realized all the difference, the gulf of difference between lines like:

> En l'an trentiesme de mon aage
> Que toutes mes hontes j'ay beues;

and even the very best of Ronsard or Bellay, such as:

> Le temps s'en va, le temps s'en va, madame;
> Las! le temps, non, mais nous nous en allons
> Et tost serons estendus sous la lame.

We should not gather from Wyndham's essay that the *Phœnix and Turtle* is a great poem, far finer than *Venus and Adonis;* but what he says about *Venus and Adonis* is worth reading, for Wyndham is very sharp in perceiving the neglected beauties of the second-rate. There is nothing to show the gulf of difference between Shakespeare's sonnets and those of any other Elizabethan. Wyndham overrates Sidney, and in his references to Elizabethan writings on the theory of poetry omits mention of the essay by Campion, an abler and more daring though less common-sense study than Daniel's. He speaks a few words for Drayton, but has not noticed that the only good lines (with the exception of one sonnet which may be an accident) in Drayton's dreary sequence of "Ideas" occur when Drayton drops his costume for a moment and talks in terms of actuality:

> Lastly, mine eyes amazedly have seen
> Essex' great fall; Tyrone his peace to gain;
> The quiet end of that long-living queen;
> The king's fair entry, and our peace with Spain.

More important than the lack of balance is the lack of critical analysis. Wyndham had, as was indicated, a gusto for the Elizabethans. His essay on the Poems of Shakespeare contains an extraordinary amount of information. There is some interesting gossip about Mary Fitton and a good anecdote of Sir William Knollys. But Wyndham misses what is the cardinal point in criticizing the Elizabethans: we cannot grasp them, understand them, without understanding of the pathology of rhetoric. Rhetoric, a particular form of rhetoric, was endemic, it pervaded the whole organism; the healthy as well as the morbid tissues were built up on it. We cannot grapple with even the simplest and most conversational lines in Tudor and early Stuart drama without having diagnosed the rhetoric in the sixteenth and seventeenth-century mind. Even when we come across lines like:

> There's a plumber laying pipes in my guts, it scalds,

we must not allow ourselves to forget the rhetorical basis any more than when we read:

> Come, let us march against the powers of heaven
> And set black streamers in the firmament
> To signify the slaughter of the gods.

An understanding of Elizabethan rhetoric is as essential to the appreciation of Elizabethan literature as an understanding of Victorian sentiment is essential to the appreciation of Victorian literature and of George Wyndham.

Wyndham was a Romantic; the only cure for Romanticism is to analyse it. What is permanent and good in Romanticism is curiosity—

> ... l' ardore
> Ch' i' ebbe a divenir del mondo esperto
> E degli vizii umani e del valore—

a curiosity which recognizes that any life, if accurately and profoundly penetrated, is interesting and always strange. Romanticism is a short cut to the strangeness without the reality, and it leads its disciples only back upon themselves. George Wyndham had curiosity, but he employed it romantically, not to penetrate the real world, but to complete the varied features of the world he made for himself. It would be of interest to divagate from literature to politics and inquire to what extent Romanticism is incorporate in Imperialism; to inquire to what extent Romanticism has possessed the imagination of Imperialists, and to what extent it was made use of by Disraeli. But this is quite another matter: there may be a good deal to be said for Romanticism in life, there is no place for it in letters. Not that we need conclude that a man of George Wyndham's antecedents and traditions must inevitably be a Romanticist writer. But this is the case when such a man plants himself firmly in his awareness of caste, when he says "The gentry must not abdicate." In politics this may be an admirable formula. It will not do in literature. The Arts insist that a man shall dispose of all that he has, even of his family tree, and follow art alone. For they require that a man be not a member of a family or of a caste or of a party or of a coterie, but simply and solely himself. A man like Wyndham brings several virtues into literature. But there is only one man better and more uncommon than the patrician, and that is the Individual.

THE LOCAL FLAVOUR

In a world which is chiefly occupied with the task of keeping up to date with itself, it is a satisfaction to know that there is at least one man who has not only read but enjoyed, and not only enjoyed but read, such authors as Petronius and Herondas. That is Mr. Charles Whibley, and there are two statements to make about him: that he is not a critic, and that he is something which is almost as rare, if not quite as precious. He has apparently read and enjoyed a great deal of English literature, and the part of it that he has most enjoyed is the literature of the great ages, the sixteenth and seventeenth centuries. We may opine that Mr. Whibley has not uttered a single important original judgment upon any of this literature. On the other hand, how many have done so? Mr. Whibley is not a critic of men or of books; but he convinces us that if we read the books that he has read we should find them as delightful as he has found them; and if we read them we can form our own opinions. And if he has not the balance of the critic, he has some other equipoise of his own. It is partly that his tastes are not puritanical, that he can talk about Restoration dramatists and others without apologizing for their "indecency"; it is partly his sense for the best local and temporal flavours; it is partly his healthy appetite.

A combination of non-critical, rather than uncritical, qualities made Mr. Whibley the most appropriate person in the world for the work by which he is best known. We should be more grateful for the "Tudor Translations Series" if we could find copies to be bought, and if we could afford to buy them when we found them. But that is not Mr. Whibley's fault. The introductions which he wrote for some of the translators are all that such introductions should be. His Urquhart's *Rabelais* contains all the irrelevant information about that writer which is what is wanted to stimulate a taste for him. After reading the introduction, to read Urquhart was the only pleasure in life. And therefore, in a country destitute of living criticism, Mr. Whibley is a useful person: for the first thing is that English literature should be read at all. The few people who talk intelligently about Stendhal and Flaubert and James know this; but the larger number of people who skim the conversation of the former do not know enough of English literature to be even insular. There are two ways in which a writer may lead us to profit by the work of dead writers. One is by isolating the essential, by pointing out the most intense in various kinds and separating it from the accidents of environment. This method is helpful only to the more intelligent people, who are capable of a unique enjoyment of perfect expression, and it concentrates on the very best in any art. The other method, that of Mr. Whibley, is to communicate a taste for the period—and for the best of the period so far as it is of that period. That is not very easy either. For a pure journalist will not know any period well enough; a pure dilettante will know it too egotistically, as a fashion of his own. Mr. Whibley is really interested; and he has escaped, without any programme of revolt, from the present century into those of Tudor and Stuart. He escapes, and perhaps leads others, by virtue of a taste which is not exactly a literary taste.

The "Tudor Translations" form part of a pronounced taste. Some are better written than others. There is, of course, a world of difference—of which Mr. Whibley is perhaps unaware—between even Florio and his original. The French of Montaigne is a mature language, and the English of Florio's living translation is not. Montaigne could be translated into the English of his time, but a similar work could not have been written in it. But as the English language matured it lost something that Florio and all his inferior colleagues had, and that they had in common with the language of Montaigne. It was not only the language, but the time. The prose of that age had life, a life to which later ages could not add, from which they could only take away. You find the same life, the same abundance, in Montaigne and Brantôme, the alteration in Rochefoucauld as in Hobbes, the desiccation in the classic prose of both languages, in Voltaire and in Gibbon. Only, the French was originally richer and more mature—already in Joinville and Commines—and we have no prose to compare with Montaigne and Rabelais. If Mr. Whibley had analysed this vitality, and told us why Holland and Underdowne, Nashe and Martin Marprelate are still worth reading, then he could have shown us how to recognize this quality when it, or something like it, appears in our own lifetime. But Mr. Whibley is not an analyst. His taste, even, becomes less certain as he fixes it on individuals within his period. On Surrey's blank verse he is feeble; he does not even give Surrey the credit of having anticipated some of Tennyson's best effects. He has no praise for Golding, quite one of the best of the verse translators; he apologizes for him by saying that Ovid demands no strength or energy! There is strength and energy, at least, in Marlowe's *Amores.* And he omits mention of Gawain Douglas, who, though he wrote in Scots, was surely a "Tudor" translator. Characteristically, Mr. Whibley praises Chapman because

> it gives proof of an abounding life, a quenchless energy. There is a grandeur and spirit in Chapman's rendering, not unworthy the original . . .

This is commonplace, and it is uncritical. And a critic would not use so careless a phrase as "Tasso's masterpiece." The essay on Congreve does not add much to our understanding:

> And so he set upon the boards a set of men and women of quick brains and cynical humours, who talked with the brilliance and rapidity wherewith the finished swordsman fences.

We have heard of this conversation like fencing before. And the suspicion is in our breast that Mr. Whibley might admire

George Meredith. The essay on Ralegh gives still less. The reality of that pleasing pirate and monopolist has escaped, and only the national hero is left. And yet Ralegh, and Swift, and Congreve, and the underworld of sixteenth and seventeenth-century letters, are somehow kept alive by what Mr. Whibley says of them.

Accordingly, Mr. Whibley does not disappear in the jungle of journalism and false criticism; he deserves a "place upon the shelves" of those who care for English literature. He has the first requisite of a critic: interest in his subject, and ability to communicate an interest in it. His defects are both of intellect and feeling. He has no dissociative faculty. There were very definite vices and definite shortcomings and immaturities in the literature he admires; and as he is not the person to tell us of the vices and shortcomings, he is not the person to lay before us the work of absolutely the finest quality. He exercises neither of the tools of the critic: comparison and analysis. He has not the austerity of passion which can detect unerringly the transition from work of eternal intensity to work that is merely beautiful, and from work that is beautiful to work that is merely charming. For the critic needs to be able not only to saturate himself in the spirit and the fashion of a time—the local flavour—but also to separate himself suddenly from it in appreciation of the highest creative work.

And he needs something else that Mr. Whibley lacks: a creative interest, a focus upon the immediate future. The important critic is the person who is absorbed in the present problems of art, and who wishes to bring the forces of the past to bear upon the solution of these problems. If the critic consider Congreve, for instance, he will have always at the back of his mind the question: What has Congreve got that is pertinent to our dramatic art? Even if he is solely engaged in trying to understand Congreve, this will make all the difference: inasmuch as to understand anything is to understand from a point of view. Most critics have some creative interest—it may be, instead of an interest in any art, an interest

(like Mr. Paul More's) in morals. These remarks were intro-
duced only to assist in giving the books of Mr. Whibley a
place, a particular but unticketed place, neither with criti-
cism, nor with history, nor with plain journalism; and the
trouble would not have been taken if the books were not
thought to be worth placing.

A NOTE ON THE AMERICAN CRITIC

This gallery of critics is not intended to be in any sense com-
plete. But having dealt with three English writers of what
may be called critical prose, one's mind becomes conscious of
the fact that they have something in common, and, trying to
perceive more clearly what this community is, and suspecting
that it is a national quality, one is impelled to meditate upon
the strongest contrast possible. Hence these comments upon
two American critics and one French critic, which would not
take exactly this form without the contrast at which I have
hinted.

Mr. Paul More is the author of a number of volumes which
he perhaps hopes will break the record of mass established by
the complete works of Sainte-Beuve. The comparison with
Sainte-Beuve is by no means trivial, for Mr. More, and Pro-
fessor Irving Babbitt also, are admirers of the voluminous
Frenchman. Not only are they admirers, but their admiration
is perhaps a clue both to much of their merit and to some of
their defects. In the first place, both of these writers have
given much more attention to French criticism, to the study
of French standards of writing and of thought, than any of
the notable English critics since Arnold; they are therefore
much nearer to the European current, although they exhibit
faults which are definitely transatlantic and which definitely
keep them out of it. The French influence is traceable in their
devotion to ideas and their interest in problems of art and life
as problems which exist and can be handled apart from their
relations to the critic's private temperament. With Swin-

burne, the criticism of Elizabethan literature has the interest
of a passion, it has the interest for us of any writing by an in-
tellectual man who is genuinely moved by certain poetry.
Swinburne's intelligence is not defective, it is impure. There
are few ideas in Swinburne's critical writings which stand
forth luminous with an independent life of their own, so true
that one forgets the author in the statement. Swinburne's
words must always be referred back to Swinburne himself.
And if literature is to Swinburne merely a passion, we are
tempted to say that to George Wyndham it was a hobby, and
to Mr. Whibley almost a charming showman's show (we are
charmed by the urbanity of the showman). The two latter
have gusto, but gusto is no equivalent for taste; it depends too
much upon the appetite and the digestion of the feeder. And
with one or two other writers, whom I have not had occasion
to discuss, literature is not so much a collection of valuable
porcelain as an institution—accepted, that is to say, with the
same gravity as the establishments of Church and State. That
is, in other words, the essentially uncritical attitude. In all of
these attitudes the English critic is the victim of his tempera-
ment. He may acquire great erudition, but erudition easily
becomes a hobby; it is useless unless it enables us to see liter-
ature all round, to detach it from ourselves, to reach a state of
pure contemplation.

Now Mr. More and Mr. Babbitt have endeavoured to es-
tablish a criticism which should be independent of tempera-
ment. This is in itself a considerable merit. But at this point
Mr. More particularly has been led astray, oddly enough, by
his guide Sainte-Beuve. Neither Mr. More nor Sainte-Beuve
is primarily interested in art. Of the latter M. Benda has well
observed that

on sait—et c'est certainement un des grands éléments de son
succès—combien d'études l'illustre critique consacre à des au-
teurs dont l'importance littéraire est quasi nulle (femmes, magis-
trats, courtisans, militaires), mais dont les écrits lui sont une

occasion de pourtraiturer une âme; combien volontiers, pour les maîtres, il s'attache à leurs productions secondaires, notes, brouillons, lettres intimes, plutôt qu'à leurs grandes œuvres, souvent beaucoup moins expressives, en effet, de leur psychologie.

Mr. More is not, like Sainte-Beuve, primarily interested in psychology or in human beings; Mr. More is primarily a moralist, which is a worthy and serious thing to be. The trouble with Mr. More is that you cannot disperse a theory or point of view of morals over a vast number of essays on a great variety of important figures in literature, unless you can give some more particular interest as well. Sainte-Beuve has his particularized interest in human beings; another critic—say Remy de Gourmont—may have something to say always about the art of a writer which will make our enjoyment of that writer more conscious and more intelligent. But the pure moralist in letters—the moralist is useful to the creator as well as the reader of poetry—must be more concise, for we must have the pleasure of inspecting the beauty of his structure. And here M. Julien Benda has a great advantage over Mr. More; his thought may be less profound, but it has more formal beauty.

Mr. Irving Babbitt, who shares so many of the ideals and opinions of Mr. More that their names must be coupled, has expressed his thought more abstractly and with more form, and is free from a mystical impulse which occasionally gets out of Mr. More's hand. He appears, more clearly than Mr. More, and certainly more clearly than any critic of equal authority in America or England, to perceive Europe as a whole; he has the cosmopolitan mind and tendency to seek the centre. His few books are important, and would be more important if he preached of discipline in a more disciplined style. Although he also is an admirer of Sainte-Beuve, he would probably subscribe to this admirable paragraph of Othenin d'Haussonville:[1]

---

[1] *Revue des Deux Mondes,* fevr. 1875, quoted by Benda, *Belphégor,* p. 140.

Il y a une beauté littéraire, impersonnelle en quelque sorte, par-
faitement distincte de l'auteur lui-même et de son organisation,
beauté qui a sa raison d'être et ses lois, dont la critique est tenue
de rendre compte. Et si la critique considère cette tâche comme
au-dessous d'elle, si c'est affaire à la rhétorique et à ce que
Sainte-Beuve appelle dédaigneusement les Quintilien, alors la
rhetorique a du bon et les Quintilien ne sont pas à dédaigner.

There may be several critics in England who would applaud
this notion; there are very few who show any evidence of its
apprehension in their writings. But Mr. More and Mr. Babbitt,
whatever their actual tastes, and although they are not pri-
marily occupied with art, are on the side of the artist. And the
side of the artist is not the side which in England is often as-
sociated with critical writing. As Mr. More has pointed out in
an interesting essay, there is a vital weakness in Arnold's def-
inition of criticism as "the disinterested endeavour to know
the best that is known and thought in the world, irrespectively
of practice, politics, and everything of the kind." The "disin-
terested endeavour to know" is only a prerequisite of the
critic, and is not *criticism,* which may be the result of such an
endeavour. Arnold states the work of the critic merely in
terms of the personal ideal, an ideal for oneself—and an ideal
for oneself is not disinterested. Here Arnold is the Briton
rather than the European.

Mr. More indicates his own attitude in praising those
whom he elevates to the position of masters of criticism:

> If they deal much with the criticism of literature, this is because
> in literature more manifestly than anywhere else life displays its
> infinitely varied motives and results; and their practice is always
> to render literature itself more consciously a criticism of life.

"Criticism of life" is a facile phrase, and at most only repre-
sents one aspect of great literature, if it does not assign to the
term "criticism" itself a generality which robs it of precision.

Mr. More has, it seems to me, in this sentence just failed to put his finger on the right seriousness of great literary art: the seriousness which we find in Villon's *Testament* and which is conspicuously absent from *In Memoriam;* or the seriousness which controls *Amos Barton* and not *The Mill on the Floss.*

It is a pity that Mr. More does not write a little oftener about the great literary artists, it is a pity that he takes the reputations of the world too solemnly. This is probably due in part to remoteness in space from the European centre. But it must be observed that English solemnity and American solemnity are very different. I do not propose to analyse the difference (it would be a valuable chapter in social history); the American solemnity, it is enough to say, is more primitive, more academic, more like that of the German professor. But it is not the fault of Mr. More or Mr. Babbitt that the culture of ideas has only been able to survive in America in the unfavourable atmosphere of the university.

THE FRENCH INTELLIGENCE

As the inspection of types of English irresistibly provoked a glance at two American critics, so the inspection of the latter leads our attention to the French. M. Julien Benda has the formal beauty which the American critics lack, and a close affinity to them in point of view. He restricts himself, perhaps, to a narrower field of ideas, but within that field he manipulates the ideas with a very exceptional cogency and clarity. To notice his last book (*Belphégor: essai sur l'esthétique de la présente société française*) would be to quote from it. M. Benda is not like Remy de Gourmont, the critical consciousness of a generation, he could not supply the conscious formulas of a sensibility in process of formation; he is rather the ideal scavenger of the rubbish of our time. Much of his analysis of the decadence of contemporary French society could be applied to London, although differences are observable from his diagnosis.

Quant à la société en elle-même, on peut prévoir que ce soin qu'elle met à éprouver de l'émoi par l'art, devenant cause à son tour, y rendra la soif de ce plaisir de plus en plus intense, l'application à la satisfaire de plus en plus jalouse et plus perfectionnée. On entrevoit le jour où la bonne société française repudiera encore le peu qu'elle supporte aujourd'hui d'idées et d'organisation dans l'art, et ne se passionera plus que pour des gestes de comédiens, pour des impressions de femmes ou d'enfants, pour des rugissements de lyriques, pour des extases de fanatiques ...

Almost the only person who has ever figured in England and attempted a task at all similar to that of M. Benda is Matthew Arnold. Matthew Arnold was intelligent, and by so much difference as the presence of one intelligent man makes, our age is inferior to that of Arnold. But what an advantage a man like M. Benda has over Arnold. It is not simply that he has a critical tradition behind him, and that Arnold is using a language which constantly tempts the user away from dispassionate exposition into sarcasm and diatribe, a language less fitted for criticism than the English of the eighteenth century. It is that the follies and stupidities of the French, no matter how base, express themselves in the form of ideas—Bergsonism itself is an intellectual construction, and the mondaines who attended lectures at the College de France were in a sense using their minds. A man of ideas needs ideas, or pseudo-ideas, to fight against. And Arnold lacked the active resistance which is necessary to keep a mind at its sharpest.

A society in which a mind like M. Benda's can exercise itself, and in which there are persons like M. Benda, is one which facilitates the task of the creative artist. M. Benda cannot be attached, like Gourmont, to any creative group. He does not wholly partake in that "conscious creation of the field of the present out of the past" which Mr. More considers to be part of the work of the critic. But in analysing the maladies of the second-rate or corrupt literature of the time he makes the labour of the creative artist lighter. The Charles

Louis Philippes of English literature are never done with, because there is no one to kill their reputations; we still hear that George Meredith is a master of prose, or even a profound philosopher. The creative artist in England finds himself compelled, or at least tempted, to spend much of his time and energy in criticism that he might reserve for the perfecting of his proper work: simply because there is no one else to do it.

TRADITION AND THE
INDIVIDUAL TALENT

I

In English writing we seldom speak of tradition, though we occasionally apply its name in deploring its absence. We cannot refer to "the tradition" or to "a tradition"; at most, we employ the adjective in saying that the poetry of So-and-so is "traditional" or even "too traditional." Seldom, perhaps, does the word appear except in a phrase of censure. If otherwise, it is vaguely approbative, with the implication, as to the work approved, of some pleasing archæological reconstruction. You can hardly make the word agreeable to English ears without this comfortable reference to the reassuring science of archæology.

Certainly the word is not likely to appear in our appreciations of living or dead writers. Every nation, every race, has not only its own creative, but its own critical turn of mind; and is even more oblivious of the shortcomings and limitations of its critical habits than of those of its creative genius. We know, or think we know, from the enormous mass of critical writing that has appeared in the French language the critical method or habit of the French; we only conclude (we are such unconscious people) that the French are "more critical" than we, and sometimes even plume ourselves a little with the fact, as if the French were the less spontaneous. Perhaps they are; but we might remind ourselves that criticism is as inevitable as breathing, and that we should be none the worse for articulating what passes in our minds when we read a book and feel an emotion about it, for criticizing our own minds in their work of criticism. One of the facts that might come to light in this process is our tendency to insist, when we praise a poet, upon those aspects of his work in which he least resembles anyone else. In these aspects or parts of his work we pretend to find what is individual, what is the peculiar essence of the man. We dwell with satisfaction upon the poet's difference from his predecessors, especially his immediate predecessors; we endeavour to find something that can be isolated in order to be enjoyed. Whereas if we approach a poet without his prejudice we shall often find that not only the best, but the most individual parts of his work may be those in which the dead poets, his ancestors, assert their immortality most vigorously. And I do not mean the impressionable period of adolescence, but the period of full maturity.

Yet if the only form of tradition, of handing down, consisted in following the ways of the immediate generation before us in a blind or timid adherence to its successes, "tradition" should positively be discouraged. We have seen many such simple currents soon lost in the sand; and novelty is better than repetition. Tradition is a matter of much wider significance. It cannot be inherited, and if you want it you must obtain it by great labour. It involves, in the first place, the historical sense, which we may call nearly indispensable to anyone who would continue to be a poet beyond his twenty-fifth year; and the historical sense involves a perception, not only of the pastness of the past, but of its presence; the historical sense compels a man to write not merely with his own generation in his bones, but with a feeling that the whole of the literature of Europe from Homer and within it the whole of the literature of his own country has a simultaneous existence and composes a simultaneous order. This historical sense, which is a sense of the timeless as well as of the temporal and of the timeless and of the temporal together, is what makes a writer traditional. And it is at the same time what makes a writer most acutely conscious of his place in time, of his contemporaneity.

No poet, no artist of any art, has his complete meaning alone. His significance, his appreciation is the appreciation of his relation to the dead poets and artists. You cannot value him alone; you must set him, for contrast and comparison, among the dead. I mean this as a principle of æsthetic, not merely historical, criticism. The necessity that he shall conform, that he shall cohere, is not one-sided; what happens when a new work of art is created is something that happens simultaneously to all the works of art which preceded it. The existing monuments form an ideal order among themselves, which is modified by the introduction of the new (the really new) work of art among them. The existing order is complete before the new work arrives; for order to persist after the supervention of novelty, the *whole* existing order must be, if ever so slightly, altered; and so the relations, proportions, values of each work of art toward the whole are readjusted; and this is conformity between the old and the new. Whoever has approved this idea of order, of the form of European, of English literature, will not find it preposterous that the past should be altered by the present as much as the present is directed by the past. And the poet who is aware of this will be aware of great difficulties and responsibilities.

In a peculiar sense he will be aware also that he must inevitably be judged by the standards of the past. I say judged, not amputated, by them; not judged to be as good as, or worse or better than, the dead; and certainly not judged by the canons of dead critics. It is a judgment, a comparison, in which two things are measured by each other. To conform merely would be for the new work not really to conform at all; it would not be new, and would therefore not be a work of art. And we do not quite say that the new is more valuable because it fits in; but its fitting in is a test of its value—a test, it is true, which can only be slowly and cautiously applied, for we are none of us infallible judges of conformity. We say: it appears to conform, and is perhaps individual, or it appears individual, and may conform; but we are hardly likely to find that it is one and not the other.

To proceed to a more intelligible exposition of the relation of the poet to the past: he can neither take the past as a lump, an indiscriminate bolus, nor can he form himself wholly on one or two private admirations, nor can he form himself wholly upon one preferred period. The first course is inadmissible, the second is an important experience of youth, and the third is a pleasant and highly desirable supplement. The poet must be very conscious of the main current, which does not at all flow invariably through the most distinguished reputations. He must be quite aware of the obvious fact that art never improves, but that the material of art is never quite the same. He must be aware that the mind of Europe—the mind of his own country—a mind which he learns in time to be much more important than his own private mind—is a mind which changes, and that this change is a development which abandons nothing *en route,* which does not superannuate either Shakespeare, or Homer, or the rock drawing of the Magdalenian draughtsmen. That this development, refinement perhaps, complication certainly, is not, from the point of view of the artist, any improvement. Perhaps not even an improvement from the point of view of the psychologist or not to the extent which we imagine; perhaps only in the end based upon a complication in economics and machinery. But the difference between the present and the past is that the conscious present is an awareness of the past in a way and to an extent which the past's awareness of itself cannot show.

Some one said: "The dead writers are remote from us because we *know* so much more than they did." Precisely, and they are that which we know.

I am alive to a usual objection to what is clearly part of my programme for the *métier* of poetry. The objection is that the doctrine requires a ridiculous amount of erudition (pedantry), a claim which can be rejected by appeal to the lives of poets in any pantheon. It will even be affirmed that much learning deadens or perverts poetic sensibility. While, however, we persist in believing that a poet ought to know as much as will not encroach upon his necessary receptivity and necessary laziness, it is not desirable to confine knowledge to whatever can be put into a useful shape for examinations, drawing-rooms, or the still more pretentious modes of publicity. Some can absorb knowledge, the more tardy must sweat for it. Shakespeare acquired more essential history from Plutarch than most men could from the whole British Museum. What is to be insisted upon is that the poet must develop or procure the consciousness of the past and that he should continue to develop this consciousness throughout his career.

What happens is a continual surrender of himself as he is at the moment to something which is more valuable. The progress of an artist is a continual self-sacrifice, a continual extinction of personality.

There remains to define this process of depersonalization and its relation to the sense of tradition. It is in this depersonalization that art may be said to approach the condition of science. I shall, therefore, invite you to consider, as a suggestive analogy, the action which takes place when a bit of finely filiated platinum is introduced into a chamber containing oxygen and sulphur dioxide.

II

Honest criticism and sensitive appreciation is directed not upon the poet but upon the poetry. If we attend to the confused cries of the newspaper critics and the susurrus of popular repetition that follows, we shall hear the names of poets in great numbers; if we seek not Blue-book knowledge but the enjoyment of poetry, and ask for a poem, we shall seldom find it. In the last article I tried to point out the importance of the relation of the poem to other poems by other authors, and suggested the conception of poetry as a living whole of all the poetry that has ever been written. The other aspect of this Impersonal theory of poetry is the relation of the poem to its author. And I hinted, by an analogy, that the mind of the mature poet differs from that of the immature one not precisely in any valuation of "personality," not being necessarily more interesting, or having "more to say," but rather by being a more finely perfected medium in which special, or very varied, feelings are at liberty to enter into new combinations.

The analogy was that of the catalyst. When the two gases previously mentioned are mixed in the presence of a filament of platinum, they form sulphurous acid. This combination takes place only if the platinum is present; nevertheless the newly formed acid contains no trace of platinum, and the platinum itself is apparently unaffected; has remained inert, neutral, and unchanged. The mind of the poet is the shred of platinum. It may partly or exclusively operate upon the experience of the man himself; but, the more perfect the artist, the more completely separate in him will be the man who suffers and the mind which creates; the more perfectly will the mind digest and transmute the passions which are its material.

The experience, you will notice, the elements which enter the presence of the transforming catalyst, are of two kinds: emotions and feelings. The effect of a work of art upon the person who enjoys it is an experience different in kind from any experience not of art. It may be formed out of one emotion, or may be a combination of several; and various feelings, inhering for the writer in particular words or phrases or images, may be added to compose the final result. Or great poetry may be made without the direct use of any emotion whatever: composed out of feelings solely. Canto XV of the *Inferno* (Brunetto Latini) is a working up of the emotion evident in the situation; but the effect, though single as that of any work of art, is obtained by considerable complexity of detail. The last quatrain gives an image, a feeling attaching to an image, which "came," which did not develop simply out of what precedes, but which was probably in suspension in the poet's mind until the proper combination arrived for it to add itself to. The poet's mind is in fact a receptacle for seizing and storing up numberless feelings, phrases, images, which remain there until all the particles which can unite to form a new compound are present together.

If you compare several representative passages of the greatest poetry you see how great is the variety of types of combination, and also how completely any semi-ethical criterion of "sublimity" misses the mark. For it is not the "greatness," the intensity, of the emotions, the components, but the intensity of the artistic process, the pressure, so to speak, under which the fusion takes place, that counts. The episode of Paolo and Francesca employs a definite emotion, but the intensity of the poetry is something quite different from whatever intensity in the supposed experience it may give the impression of. It is no more intense, furthermore, than Canto XXVI, the voyage of Ulysses, which has not the direct dependence upon an emotion. Great variety is possible in the process of transmutation of emotion: the murder of Agamemnon, or the agony of Othello, gives an artistic effect apparently closer to a possible original than the scenes from Dante. In the *Agamemnon,* the artistic emotion approximates to the emotion of an actual spectator; in *Othello* to the emotion of the protagonist himself. But the difference between art and the event is always absolute; the combination which is the murder of Agamemnon is probably as complex as that which is the voyage of Ulysses. In either case there has been a fusion of elements. The ode of Keats contains a number of feelings which have nothing particular to do with the nightingale, but which the nightingale, partly, perhaps, because of its attractive name, and partly because of its reputation, served to bring together.

The point of view which I am struggling to attack is perhaps related to the metaphysical theory of the substantial unity of the soul: for my meaning is, that the poet has, not a "personality" to express, but a particular medium, which is only a medium and not a personality, in which impressions and experiences combine in peculiar and unexpected ways. Impressions and experiences which are important for the man may take no place in the poetry, and those which become important in the poetry may play quite a negligible part in the man, the personality.

I will quote a passage which is unfamiliar enough to be regarded with fresh attention in the light—or darkness—of these observations:

> And now methinks I could e'en chide myself
> For doating on her beauty, though her death
> Shall be revenged after no common action.
> Does the silkworm expend her yellow labours
> For thee? For thee does she undo herself?
> Are lordships sold to maintain ladyships
> For the poor benefit of a bewildering minute?
> Why does yon fellow falsify highways,
> And put his life between the judge's lips,
> To refine such a thing—keeps horse and men
> To beat their valours for her? . . .

In this passage (as is evident if it is taken in its context) there is a combination of positive and negative emotions: an intensely strong attraction toward beauty and an equally intense fascination by the ugliness which is contrasted with it and which destroys it. This balance of contrasted emotion is in the dramatic situation to which the speech is pertinent, but that situation alone is inadequate to it. This is, so to speak, the structural emotion, provided by the drama. But the whole effect, the dominant tone, is due to the fact that a number of floating feelings, having an affinity to this emotion by no means superficially evident, have combined with it to give us a new art emotion.

It is not in his personal emotions, the emotions provoked by particular events in his life, that the poet is in any way remarkable or interesting. His particular emotions may be simple, or crude, or flat. The emotion in his poetry will be a very complex thing, but not with the complexity of the emotions of people who have very complex or unusual emotions in life. One error, in fact, of eccentricity in poetry is to seek for new human emotions to express: and in this search for novelty in the wrong place it discovers the perverse. The business of the poet is not to find new emotions, but to use the ordinary ones and, in working them up into poetry, to express feelings which are not in actual emotions at all. And emotions which he has never experienced will serve his turn as well as those familiar to him. Consequently, we must believe that "emotion recollected in tranquillity" is an inexact formula. For it is neither emotion, nor recollection, nor, without distortion of meaning, tranquillity. It is a concentration, and a new thing resulting from the concentration, of a very great number of experiences which to the practical and active person would not seem to be experiences at all; it is a concentration which does not happen consciously or of deliberation. These experiences are not "recollected," and they finally unite in an atmosphere which is "tranquil" only in that it is a passive attending upon the event. Of course this is not quite the whole story. There is a great deal, in the writing of poetry, which must be conscious and deliberate. In fact, the bad poet is usually unconscious where he ought to be conscious, and conscious where he ought to be unconscious. Both errors tend to make him "personal." Poetry is not a turning loose of emotion, but an escape from emotion; it is not the expression of personality, but an escape from personality. But, of course, only those who have personality and emotions know what it means to want to escape from these things.

III

ὁ δὲ νοῦς ἴσως θειότερόν τι καὶ ἀπαθές ἐστιν

This essay proposes to halt at the frontier of metaphysics or mysticism, and confine itself to such practical conclusions as can be applied by the responsible person interested in poetry.

To divert interest from the poet to the poetry is a laudable aim: for it would conduce to a juster estimation of actual poetry, good and bad. There are many people who appreciate the expression of sincere emotion in verse, and there is a smaller number of people who can appreciate technical excellence. But very few know when there is expression of *significant* emotion, emotion which has its life in the poem and not in the history of the poet. The emotion of art is impersonal. And the poet cannot reach this impersonality without surrendering himself wholly to the work to be done. And he is not likely to know what is to be done unless he lives in what is not merely the present, but the present moment of the past, unless he is conscious, not of what is dead, but of what is already living.

THE POSSIBILITY OF A
POETIC DRAMA

The questions—why there is no poetic drama to-day, how the stage has lost all hold on literary art, why so many poetic plays are written which can only be read, and read, if at all, without pleasure—have become insipid, almost academic. The usual conclusion is either that "conditions" are too much for us, or that we really prefer other types of literature, or simply that we are uninspired. As for the last alternative, it is not to be entertained; as for the second, what type do we prefer?; and as for the first, no one has ever shown me "conditions," except of the most superficial. The reasons for raising the question again are first that the majority, perhaps, certainly a large number, of poets hanker for the stage; and second, that a not negligible public appears to want verse plays. Surely there is some legitimate craving, not restricted to a few persons, which only the verse play can satisfy. And surely the critical attitude is to attempt to analyse the conditions and the other data. If there comes to light some conclusive obstacle, the investigation should at least help us to turn our thoughts to more profitable pursuits; and if there is not, we may hope to arrive eventually at some statement of conditions which might be altered. Possibly we shall find that our incapacity has a deeper source: the arts have at times flourished when there was no drama; possibly we are incompetent altogether; in that case the stage will be, not the seat, but at all events a symptom, of the malady.

From the point of view of literature, the drama is only one among several poetic forms. The epic, the ballad, the chanson de geste, the forms of Provence and of Tuscany, all found their perfection by serving particular societies. The forms of Ovid, Catullus, Propertius, served a society different, and in some respects more civilized, than any of these; and in the society of Ovid the drama as a form of art was comparatively insignificant. Nevertheless, the drama is perhaps the most permanent, is capable of greater variation and of expressing more varied types of society, than any other. It varied considerably in England alone; but when one day it was discovered lifeless, subsequent forms which had enjoyed a transitory life were dead too. I am not prepared to undertake the historical survey; but I should say that the poetic drama's autopsy was performed as much by Charles Lamb as by anyone else. For a form is not wholly dead until it is known to be; and Lamb, by exhuming the remains of dramatic life at its fullest, brought a consciousness of the immense gap between present and past. It was impossible to believe, after that, in a dramatic "tradition." The relation of Byron's *English Bards* and the poems of Crabbe to the work of Pope was a continuous tradition; but the relation of *The Cenci* to the great English drama is almost that of a reconstruction to an original. By losing tradition, we lose our hold on the present; but so far as there was any dramatic tradition in Shelley's day there was nothing worth the keeping. There is all the difference between preservation and restoration.

The Elizabethan Age in England was able to absorb a great quantity of new thoughts and new images, almost dispensing with tradition, because it had this great form of its own which imposed itself on everything that came to it. Consequently, the blank verse of their plays accomplished a subtlety and consciousness, even an intellectual power, that no blank verse since has developed or even repeated; elsewhere this age is crude, pedantic, or loutish in comparison with its contemporary France or Italy. The nineteenth century had a good many fresh impressions; but it had no form in which to confine them. Two men, Wordsworth and Browning, hammered out forms for themselves—personal forms, *The Excursion, Sordello, The Ring and the Book, Dramatic Monologues;* but no man can invent a form, create a taste for it, and perfect it too. Tennyson, who might unquestionably have been a consummate master of minor forms, took to turning out large patterns on a machine. As for Keats and Shelley, they were too young to be judged, and they were trying one form after another.

These poets were certainly obliged to consume vast energy in this pursuit of form, which could never lead to a wholly satisfying result. There has only been one Dante; and, after all, Dante had the benefit of years of practice in forms employed and altered by numbers of contemporaries and predecessors; he did not waste the years of youth in metric invention; and when he came to the *Commedia* he knew how to pillage right and left. To have, given into one's hands, a crude form, capable of indefinite refinement, and to be the person to see the possibilities—Shakespeare was very fortunate. And it is perhaps the craving for some such *donnée* which draws us on toward the present mirage of poetic drama.

But it is now very questionable whether there are more than two or three in the present generation who are *capable,* the least little bit, of benefiting by such advantages were they given. At most two or three actually devote themselves to this pursuit of form for which they have little or no public recognition. To create a form is not merely to invent a shape, a rhyme or rhythm. It is also the realization of the whole appropriate content of this rhyme or rhythm. The sonnet of Shakespeare is not merely such and such a pattern, but a precise way of thinking and feeling. The *framework* which was provided for the Elizabethan dramatist was not merely blank verse and the five-act play and the Elizabethan playhouse; it was not merely the plot—for the poets incorporated, remodelled, adapted or invented, as occasion suggested. It was also the half-formed ῾ὕλή, the "temper of the age" (an unsatisfactory phrase), a preparedness, a habit on the part of the public, to respond to particular stimuli. There is a book to be written on the commonplaces of any great dramatic period, the handling of Fate or Death, the recurrence of mood, tone, situation. We should see then just how *little* each poet had to do; only so much as would make a play his, only what was really essential to make it different from anyone else's. When there is this economy of effort it is possible to have several, even many, good poets at once. The great ages did not perhaps *produce* much more talent than ours; but less talent was wasted.

Now in a formless age there is very little hope for the minor poet to do anything worth doing; and when I say minor I mean very good poets indeed: such as filled the Greek anthology and the Elizabethan songbooks; even a Herrick; but not merely second-rate poets, for Denham and Waller have quite another importance, occupying points in the development of a major form. When everything is set out for the minor poet to do, he may quite frequently come upon some *trouvaille*, even in the drama: Peele and Brome are examples. Under the present conditions, the minor poet has too much to do. And this leads to another reason for the incompetence of our time in poetic drama.

Permanent literature is always a presentation: either a presentation of thought, or a presentation of feeling by a statement of events in human action or objects in the external world. In earlier literature—to avoid the word "classic"—we find both kinds, and sometimes, as in some of the dialogues of Plato, exquisite combinations of both. Aristotle presents thought, stripped to the essential structure, and he is a great *writer.* The *Agamemnon* or *Macbeth* is equally a statement, but of events. They are as much works of the "intellect" as the writings of Aristotle. There are more recent works of art which have the same quality of intellect in common with those of Æschylus and Shakespeare and Aristotle: *Education Sentimen-*

tale is one of them. Compare it with such a book as *Vanity Fair* and you will see that the labour of the intellect consisted largely in a purification, in keeping out a great deal that Thackeray allowed to remain in; in refraining from reflection, in putting into the statement enough to make reflection unnecessary. The case of Plato is still more illuminating. Take the *Theætetus*. In a few opening words Plato gives a scene, a personality, a feeling, which colour the subsequent discourse but do not interfere with it: the particular setting, and the abstruse theory of knowledge afterwards developed, co-operate without confusion. Could any contemporary author exhibit such control?

In the nineteenth century another mentality manifested itself. It is evident in a very able and brilliant poem, Goethe's *Faust*. Marlowe's Mephistopheles is a simpler creature than Goethe's. But at least Marlowe has, in a few words, concentrated him into a statement. He is there, and (incidentally) he renders Milton's Satan superfluous. Goethe's demon inevitably sends us back to Goethe. He embodies a philosophy. A creation of art should not do that: he should *replace* the philosophy. Goethe has not, that is to say, sacrificed or consecrated his thought to make the drama; the drama is still a means. And this type of mixed art has been repeated by men incomparably smaller than Goethe. We have had one other remarkable work of this type: *Peer Gynt*. And we have had the plays of M. Maeterlinck and M. Claudel.[1]

In the work of Maeterlinck and Claudel on the one hand, and those of M. Bergson on the other, we have the mixture of the genres in which our age delights. Every work of imagination must have a philosophy; and every philosophy must be a work of art—how often have we heard that M. Bergson is an

[1] I should except *The Dynasts*. This gigantic panorama is hardly to be called a success, but it is essentially an attempt to present a vision, and "sacrifices" the philosophy to the vision, as all great dramas do. Mr. Hardy has apprehended his matter as a poet and an artist.

artist! It is a boast of his disciples. It is what the word "art" means to them that is the disputable point. Certain works of philosophy can be called works of art: much of Aristotle and Plato, Spinoza, parts of Hume, Mr. Bradley's *Principles of Logic,* Mr. Russell's essay on "Denoting": clear and beautifully formed thought. But this is not what the admirers of Bergson, Claudel, or Maeterlinck (the philosophy of the latter is a little out of date) mean. They mean precisely what is not clear, but what is an emotional stimulus. And as a mixture of thought and of vision provides more stimulus, by suggesting both, both clear thinking and clear statement of particular objects must disappear.

The undigested "idea" or philosophy, the idea-emotion, is to be found also in poetic dramas which are conscientious attempts to adapt a true structure, Athenian or Elizabethan, to contemporary feeling. It appears sometimes as the attempt to supply the defect of structure by an internal structure. "But most important of all is the structure of the incidents. For Tragedy is an imitation, not of men, but of an action and of life, and life consists in action, and its end is a mode of action, not a quality."[1]

We have on the one hand the "poetic" drama, imitation Greek, imitation Elizabethan, or modern-philosophical, on the other the comedy of "ideas," from Shaw to Galsworthy, down to the ordinary social comedy. The most ramshackle Guitry farce has some paltry idea or comment upon life put into the mouth of one of the characters at the end. It is said that the stage can be used for a variety of purposes, that in only one of them perhaps is it united with literary art. A mute theatre is a possibility (I do not mean the cinema); the ballet is an actuality (though undernourished); opera is an institution; but where you have "imitations of life" on the stage, with speech, the only standard that we can allow is the standard of the work of art, aiming at the same intensity at which poetry

---

[1] *Poetics,* vi. 9. Butcher's translation.

and the other forms of art aim. From that point of view the Shavian drama is a hybrid as the Maeterlinckian drama is, and we need express no surprise at their belonging to the same epoch. Both philosophies are popularizations: the moment an idea has been transferred from its pure state in order that it may become comprehensible to the inferior intelligence it has lost contact with art. It can remain pure only by being stated simply in the form of general truth, or by being transmuted, as the attitude of Flaubert toward the small bourgeois is transformed in *Education Sentimentale.* It has there become so identified with the reality that you can no longer say what the idea is.

The essential is not, of course, that drama should be written in verse, or that we should be able to extenuate our appreciation of broad farce by occasionally attending a performance of a play of Euripides where Professor Murray's translation is sold at the door. The essential is to get upon the stage this precise statement of life which is at the same time a point of view, a world—a world which the author's mind has subjected to a complete process of simplification. I do not find that any drama which "embodies a philosophy" of the author's (like *Faust*) or which illustrates any social theory (like Shaw's) can possibly fulfil the requirements—though a place might be left for Shaw if not for Goethe. And the world of Ibsen and the world of Tchehov are not enough simplified, universal.

Finally, we must take into account the instability of any art—the drama, music, dancing—which depends upon representation by performers. The intervention of performers introduces a complication of economic conditions which is in itself likely to be injurious. A struggle, more or less unconscious, between the creator and the interpreter is almost inevitable. The interest of a performer is almost certain to be centred in himself: a very slight acquaintance with actors and musicians will testify. The performer is interested not in form but in opportunities for virtuosity or in the communication of his "personality"; the formlessness, the lack of intellectual clarity and distinction in modern music, the great physical stamina and physical training which it often requires, are perhaps signs of the triumph of the performer. The consummation of the triumph of the actor over the play is perhaps the productions of the Guitry.

The conflict is one which certainly cannot be terminated by the utter rout of the actor profession. For one thing, the stage appeals to too many demands besides the demand for art for that to be possible; and also we need, unfortunately, something more than refined automatons. Occasionally attempts have been made to "get around" the actor, to envelop him in masks, to set up a few "conventions" for him to stumble over, or even to develop little breeds of actors for some special Art drama. This meddling with nature seldom succeeds; nature usually overcomes these obstacles. Possibly the majority of attempts to confect a poetic drama have begun at the wrong end; they have aimed at the small public which wants "poetry." ("Novices," says Aristotle, "in the art attain to finish of diction and precision of portraiture before they can construct the plot.") The Elizabethan drama was aimed at a public which wanted *entertainment* of a crude sort, but would *stand* a good deal of poetry; our problem should be to take a form of entertainment, and subject it to the process which would leave it a form of art. Perhaps the music-hall comedian is the best material. I am aware that this is a dangerous suggestion to make. For every person who is likely to consider it seriously there are a dozen toymakers who would leap to tickle æsthetic society into one more quiver and giggle of art debauch. Very few treat art seriously. There are those who treat it solemnly, and will continue to write poetic pastiches of Euripides and Shakespeare; and there are others who treat it as a joke.

EURIPIDES AND
PROFESSOR MURRAY

The recent appearance of Miss Sybil Thorndyke as Medea at
the Holborn Empire is an event which has a bearing upon
three subjects of considerable interest: the drama, the present
standing of Greek literature, and the importance of good
contemporary translation. On the occasion on which I was
present the performance was certainly a success; the audience
was large, it was attentive, and its applause was long. Whether
the success was due to Euripides is uncertain; whether it was
due to Professor Murray is not proved; but that it was in con-
siderable measure due to Miss Thorndyke there is no doubt.
To have held the centre of the stage for two hours in a rôle
which requires both extreme violence and restraint, a rôle
which requires simple force and subtle variation; to have sus-
tained such a rôle almost without support; this was a legiti-
mate success. The audience, or what could be seen of it from
one of the cheaper seats, was serious and respectful and per-
haps inclined to self-approval at having attended the perfor-
mance of a Greek play; but Miss Thorndyke's acting might
have held almost any audience. It employed all the conven-
tions, the theatricalities, of the modern stage; yet her person-
ality triumphed over not only Professor Murray's verse but
her own training.

The question remains whether the production was a "work

of art." The rest of the cast appeared slightly ill at ease; the nurse was quite a tolerable nurse of the crone type; Jason was negative; the messenger was uncomfortable at having to make such a long speech; and the refined Dalcroze chorus had mellifluous voices which rendered their lyrics happily inaudible. All this contributed toward the high-brow effect which is so depressing; and we imagine that the actors of Athens, who had to speak clearly enough for 20,000 auditors to be able to criticize the versification, would have been pelted with figs and olives had they mumbled so unintelligibly as most of this troupe. But the Greek actor spoke in his own language, and our actors were forced to speak in the language of Professor Gilbert Murray. So that on the whole we may say that the performance was an interesting one.

I do not believe, however, that such performances will do very much to rehabilitate Greek literature or our own, unless they stimulate a desire for better translations. The serious auditors, many of whom I observed to be like myself provided with Professor Murray's eighteenpenny translation, were probably not aware that Miss Thorndyke, in order to succeed as well as she did, was really engaged in a struggle against the translator's verse. She triumphed over it by attracting our attention to her expression and tone and making us neglect her words; and this, of course, was not the dramatic method of Greek acting at its best. The English and Greek languages remained where they were. But few persons realize that the Greek language and the Latin language, and, *therefore,* we say, the English language, are within our lifetime passing through a critical period. The Classics have, during the latter part of the nineteenth century and up to the present moment, lost their place as a pillar of the social and political system—such as the Established Church still is. If they are to survive, to justify themselves as literature, as an element in the European mind, as the foundation for the literature we hope to create, they are very badly in need of persons capable of expounding them. We need some one—not a member of the Church of Rome, and perhaps preferably not a member of the Church of England—to explain how vital a matter it is, if Aristotle may be said to have been a moral pilot of Europe, whether we shall or shall not drop that pilot. And we need a number of educated poets who shall at least have opinions about Greek drama, and whether it is or is not of any use to us. And it must be said that Professor Gilbert Murray is not the man for this. Greek poetry will never have the slightest vitalizing effect upon English poetry if it can only appear masquerading as a vulgar debasement of the eminently personal idiom of Swinburne. These are strong words to use against the most popular Hellenist of his time; but we must witness of Professor Murray ere we die that these things are not otherwise but thus.

This is really a point of capital importance. That the most conspicuous Greek propagandist of the day should almost habitually use two words where the Greek language requires one, and where the English language will provide him with one; that he should render σκιάν by "*grey* shadow"; and that he should stretch the Greek brevity to fit the loose frame of William Morris, and blur the Greek lyric to the fluid haze of Swinburne; these are not faults of infinitesimal insignificance. The first great speech of Medea Mr. Murray begins with:

> Women of Corinth, I am come to show
> My face, lest ye despise me. . . .

We find in the Greek, ἐξῆλθον δόμων. "Show my face," therefore, is Mr. Murray's gift.

> This thing undreamed of, sudden from on high,
> Hath sapped my soul: I dazzle where I stand,
> The cup of all life shattered in my hand. . . .

Again, we find that the Greek is:

ἐμοὶ δ᾽ ἄελπτον πρᾶγμα προσπεσὸν τόδε
ψυχὴν διέφθαρκ᾽· οἴχομαι δὲ καὶ βίου
χάριν μεθεῖσα κατθανεῖν χρήζω, φίλαι.

So, here are two striking phrases which we owe to Mr. Murray; it is he who has sapped our soul and shattered the cup of all life for Euripides. And these are only random examples.

οὐκ ἔστιν ἄλλη φρὴν μιαιφονωτέρα

becomes "no bloodier spirit between heaven and hell"! Surely we know that Professor Murray is acquainted with "Sister Helen"? Professor Murray has simply interposed between Euripides and ourselves a barrier more impenetrable than the Greek language. We do not reproach him for preferring, apparently, Euripides to Æschylus. But if he does, he should at least appreciate Euripides. And it is inconceivable that anyone with a genuine feeling for the sound of Greek verse should deliberately elect the William Morris couplet, the Swinburne lyric, as a just equivalent.

As a poet, Mr. Murray is merely a very insignificant follower of the pre-Raphaelite movement. As a Hellenist, he is very much of the present day, and a very important figure in the day. This day began, in a sense, with Tylor and a few German anthropologists; since then we have acquired sociology and social psychology, we have watched the clinics of Ribot and Janet, we have read books from Vienna and heard a discourse of Bergson; a philosophy arose at Cambridge; social emancipation crawled abroad; our historical knowledge has of course increased; and we have a curious Freudian-social-mystical-rationalistic-higher-critical interpretation of the Classics and what used to be called the Scriptures. I do not deny the very great value of all work by scientists in their own departments, the great interest also of this work in detail and in its consequences. Few books are more fascinating than those of Miss Harrison, Mr. Cornford, or Mr. Cooke, when they burrow in the origins of Greek myths and rites; M. Durkheim, with his social consciousness, and M. Levy-Bruhl, with his Bororo Indians who convince themselves that they are parroquets, are delightful writers. A number of sciences have sprung up in an almost tropical exuberance which undoubtedly excites our admiration, and the garden, not unnaturally, has come to resemble a jungle. Such men as Tylor, and Robertson Smith, and Wilhelm Wundt, who early fertilized the soil, would hardly recognize the resulting vegetation; and indeed poor Wundt's *Völkerpsychologie* was a musty relic before it was translated.

All these events are useful and important in their phase, and they have sensibly affected our attitude towards the Classics; and it is this phase of classical study that Professor Murray—the friend and inspirer of Miss Jane Harrison—represents. The Greek is no longer the awe-inspiring Belvedere of Winckelmann, Goethe, and Schopenhauer, the figure of which Walter Pater and Oscar Wilde offered us a slightly debased re-edition. And we realize better how different—not how much more Olympian—were the conditions of the Greek civilization from ours; and at the same time Mr. Zimmern has shown us how the Greek dealt with analogous problems. Incidentally we do not believe that a good English prose style can be modelled upon Cicero, or Tacitus, or Thucydides. If Pindar bores us, we admit it; we are not certain that Sappho was *very* much greater than Catullus; we hold various opinions about Vergil; and we think more highly of Petronius than our grandfathers did.

It is to be hoped that we may be grateful to Professor Murray and his friends for what they have done, while we endeavour to neutralize Professor Murray's influence upon Greek literature and English language in his translations by making better translations. The choruses from Euripides by H. D. are, allowing for errors and even occasional omissions of difficult passages, much nearer to both Greek and English than Mr. Murray's. But H. D. and the other poets of the "Poets' Translation Series" have so far done no more than pick up some of the more romantic crumbs of Greek literature; none of them has yet shown himself competent to attack the *Agamemnon*. If we are to digest the heavy food of historical and scientific knowledge that we have eaten we must be prepared for much greater exertions. We need a digestion which can assimilate both Homer and Flaubert. We need a careful study of Renaissance Humanists and Translators, such as Mr. Pound has begun. We need an eye which can see the past in its place with its definite differences from the present, and yet so lively that it shall be as present to us as the present. This is the creative eye; and it is because Professor Murray has no creative instinct that he leaves Euripides quite dead.

"Rhetoric" and Poetic Drama

The death of Rostand is the disappearance of the poet whom, more than any other in France, we treated as the exponent of "rhetoric," thinking of rhetoric as something recently out of fashion. And as we find ourselves looking back rather tenderly upon the author of *Cyrano* we wonder what this vice or quality is that is associated as plainly with Rostand's merits as with his defects. His rhetoric, at least, suited him at times so well, and so much better than it suited a much greater poet, Baudelaire, who is at times as rhetorical as Rostand. And we begin to suspect that the word is merely a vague term of abuse for any style that is bad, that is so evidently bad or second-rate that we do not recognize the necessity for greater precision in the phrases we apply to it.

Our own Elizabethan and Jacobean poetry—in so nice a problem it is much safer to stick to one's own language—is repeatedly called "rhetorical." It had this and that notable quality, but, when we wish to admit that it had defects, it is rhetorical. It had serious defects, even gross faults, but we cannot be considered to have erased them from our language when we are so unclear in our perception of what they are. The fact is that both Elizabethan prose and Elizabethan poetry are written in a variety of styles with a variety of vices. Is the style of Lyly, is Euphuism, rhetorical? In contrast to the elder style of Ascham and Elyot which it assaults, it is a clear, flowing, orderly and relatively pure style, with a systematic if monotonous formula of antitheses and similes. Is the style of Nashe? A tumid, flatulent, vigorous style very different from Lyly's. Or it is perhaps the strained and the mixed figures of speech in which Shakespeare indulged himself. Or it is perhaps the careful declamation of Jonson. The word simply cannot be used as synonymous with bad writing. The meanings which it has been obliged to shoulder have been mostly opprobrious; but if a precise meaning can be found for it this meaning may occasionally represent a virtue. It is one of those words which it is the business of criticism to dissect and reassemble. Let us avoid the assumption that rhetoric is a vice of manner, and endeavour to find a rhetoric of substance also, which is right because it issues from what it has to express.

At the present time there is a manifest preference for the "conversational" in poetry—the style of "direct speech," opposed to the "oratorical" and the rhetorical; but if rhetoric is any convention of writing inappropriately applied, this conversational style can and does become a rhetoric—or what is supposed to be a conversational style, for it is often as remote from polite discourse as well could be. Much of the second and third rate in American *vers libre* is of this sort; and much of the second and third rate in English Wordsworthianism. There is in fact no conversational or other form which can be applied indiscriminately; if a writer wishes to give the effect of speech he must positively give the effect of himself talking in his own person or in one of his rôles; and if we are to express ourselves, our variety of thoughts and feelings, on a variety of subjects with inevitable rightness, we must adapt our manner to the moment with infinite variations. Examination of the development of Elizabethan drama shows this progress in adaptation, a development from monotony to variety, a progressive refinement in the perception of the variations of feeling, and a progressive elaboration of the means of expressing these variations. This drama is admitted to have grown away from the rhetorical expression, the bombast speeches, of

Kyd and Marlowe to the subtle and dispersed utterance of Shakespeare and Webster. But this apparent abandonment or outgrowth of rhetoric is two things: it is partly an improvement in language and it is partly progressive variation in feeling. There is, of course, a long distance separating the furibund fluency of old Hieronimo and the broken words of Lear. There is also a difference between the famous

> Oh eyes no eyes, but fountains full of tears!
> Oh life no life, but lively form of death!

and the superb "additions to Hieronimo."[1]

We think of Shakespeare perhaps as the dramatist who concentrates everything into a sentence, "Pray you undo this button," or "Honest honest Iago"; we forget that there is a rhetoric proper to Shakespeare at his best period which is quite free from the genuine Shakespearean vices either of the early period or the late. These passages are comparable to the best bombast of Kyd or Marlowe, with a greater command of language and a greater control of the emotion. *The Spanish Tragedy* is bombastic when it descends to language which was only the trick of its age; *Tamburlaine* is bombastic because it is monotonous, inflexible to the alterations of emotion. The really fine rhetoric of Shakespeare occurs in situations where a character in the play *sees himself* in a dramatic light:

Othello.   And say, besides,—that in Aleppo once ...

Coriolanus.   If you have writ your annals true, 'tis there,
That like an eagle in a dovecote, I
Fluttered your Volscians in Corioli.
Alone I did it.   Boy!

---

[1] Of the authorship it can only be said that the lines are by some admirer of Marlowe. This might well be Jonson.

Timon.   Come not to me again; but say to Athens,
              Timon hath made his everlasting mansion
              Upon the beachèd verge of the salt flood . . .

It occurs also once in *Antony and Cleopatra*, when Enobarbus is inspired to see Cleopatra in this dramatic light:

The barge she sat in . . .

Shakespeare made fun of Marston, and Jonson made fun of Kyd. But in Marston's play the words were expressive of nothing; and Jonson was criticizing the feeble and conceited language, not the emotion, not the "oratory." Jonson is as oratorical himself, and the moments when his oratory succeeds are, I believe, the moments that conform to our formula. Notably the speech of Sylla's ghost in the induction to *Catiline*, and the speech of Envy at the beginning of *The Poetaster.* These two figures are contemplating their own dramatic importance, and quite properly. But in the Senate speeches in *Catiline*, how tedious, how dusty! Here we are spectators not of a play of characters, but of a play of forensic, exactly as if we had been forced to attend the sitting itself. A speech in a play should never appear to be intended to move us as it might conceivably move other characters in the play, for it is essential that we should preserve our position of spectators, and observe always from the outside though with complete understanding. The scene in *Julius Cæsar* is right because the object of our attention is not the speech of Antony (*Bedeutung*) but the effect of his speech upon the mob, and Antony's intention, his preparation and consciousness of the effect. And in the rhetorical speeches from Shakespeare which have been cited, we have this necessary advantage of a new clue to the character, in noting the angle from which he views himself. But when a character *in* a play makes a direct appeal to us, we are either the victims of our own sentiment, or we are in the presence of a vicious rhetoric.

These references ought to supply some evidence of the propriety of Cyrano on Noses. Is not Cyrano exactly in this position of contemplating himself as a romantic, a dramatic figure? This dramatic sense on the part of the characters themselves is rare in modern drama. In sentimental drama it appears in a degraded form, when we are evidently intended to accept the character's sentimental interpretation of himself. In plays of realism we often find parts which are never allowed to be consciously dramatic, for fear, perhaps, of their appearing less real. But in actual life, in many of those situations in actual life which we enjoy consciously and keenly, we are at times aware of ourselves in this way, and these moments are of very great usefulness to dramatic verse. A very small part of acting is that which takes place on the stage! Rostand had—whether he had anything else or not—this dramatic sense, and it is what gives life to Cyrano. It is a sense which is almost a sense of humour (for when anyone is conscious of himself as acting, something like a sense of humour is present). It gives Rostand's characters—Cyrano at least—a gusto which is uncommon on the modern stage. No doubt Rostand's people play up to this too steadily. We recognize that in the love scenes of Cyrano in the garden, for in *Romeo and Juliet* the profounder dramatist shows his lovers melting into incoherent unconsciousness of their isolated selves, shows the human soul in the process of forgetting itself. Rostand could not do that; but in the particular case of Cyrano on Noses, the character, the situation, the occasion were perfectly suited and combined. The tirade generated by this combination is not only genuinely and highly dramatic: it is possibly poetry also. If a writer is incapable of composing such a scene as this, so much the worse for his poetic drama.

Cyrano satisfies, as far as scenes like this can satisfy, the requirements of poetic drama. It must take genuine and substantial human emotions, such emotions as observation can confirm, typical emotions, and give them artistic form; the degree of abstraction is a question for the method of each author. In Shakespeare the form is determined in the unity of the whole, as well as single scenes; it is something to attain this unity, as Rostand does, in scenes if not the whole play. Not only as a dramatist, but as a poet, he is superior to Maeterlinck, whose drama, in failing to be dramatic, fails also to be poetic. Maeterlinck has a literary perception of the dramatic and a literary perception of the poetic, and he joins the two; the two are not, as sometimes they are in the work of Rostand, fused. His characters take no conscious delight in their rôle—they are sentimental. With Rostand the centre of gravity is in the expression of the emotion, not as with Maeterlinck in the emotion which cannot be expressed. Some writers appear to believe that emotions gain in intensity through being inarticulate. Perhaps the emotions are not significant enough to endure full daylight.

In any case, we may take our choice: we may apply the term "rhetoric" to the type of dramatic speech which I have instanced, and then we must admit that it covers good as well as bad. Or we may choose to except this type of speech from rhetoric. In that case we must say that rhetoric is any adornment or inflation of speech which is *not done for a particular effect* but for a general impressiveness. And in this case, too, we cannot allow the term to cover all bad writing.

Some Notes on the Blank Verse of Christopher Marlowe

"Marloe was stabd with a dagger, and dyed swearing"

A more friendly critic, Mr. A. C. Swinburne, observes of this poet that "the father of English tragedy and the creator of English blank verse was therefore also the teacher and the guide of Shakespeare." In this sentence there are two misleading assumptions and two misleading conclusions. Kyd has as good a title to the first honour as Marlowe; Surrey has a better title to the second; and Shakespeare was not taught or guided by one of his predecessors or contemporaries alone. The less questionable judgment is, that Marlowe exercised a strong influence over later drama, though not himself as great a dramatist as Kyd; that he introduced several new tones into blank verse, and commenced the dissociative process which drew it farther and farther away from the rhythms of rhymed verse; and that when Shakespeare borrowed from him, which was pretty often at the beginning, Shakespeare either made something inferior or something different.

The comparative study of English versification at various periods is a large tract of unwritten history. To make a study of blank verse alone, would be to elicit some curious conclusions. It would show, I believe, that blank verse within Shakespeare's lifetime was more highly developed, that it became the vehicle of more varied and more intense art-emotions than it has ever conveyed since; and that after the erection of the Chinese Wall of Milton, blank verse has suffered not only arrest but retrogression. That the blank verse of Tennyson, for example, a consummate master of this form in certain applications, is cruder (*not* "rougher" or less perfect in technique) than that of half a dozen contemporaries of Shakespeare; cruder, because less capable of expressing complicated, subtle, and surprising emotions.

Every writer who has written any blank verse worth saving has produced particular tones which his verse and no other's is capable of rendering; and we should keep this in mind when we talk about "influences" and "indebtedness." Shakespeare is "universal" (if you like) because he has more of these tones than anyone else; but they are all out of the one man; one man cannot be more than one man; there might have been six Shakespeares at once without conflicting frontiers; and to say that Shakespeare expressed nearly all human emotions, implying that he left very little for anyone else, is a radical misunderstanding of art and the artist—a misunderstanding which, even when explicitly rejected, may lead to our neglecting the effort of attention necessary to discover the specific properties of the verse of Shakespeare's contemporaries. The development of blank verse may be likened to the analysis of that astonishing industrial product coal-tar. Marlowe's verse is one of the earlier derivatives, but it possesses properties which are not repeated in any of the analytic or synthetic blank verses discovered somewhat later.

The "vices of style" of Marlowe's and Shakespeare's age is a convenient name for a number of vices, no one of which, perhaps, was shared by all of the writers. It is pertinent, at least, to remark that Marlowe's "rhetoric" is not, or not characteristically, Shakespeare's rhetoric; that Marlowe's rhetoric consists in a pretty simple huffe-snuffe bombast, while Shakespeare's is more exactly a vice of style, a tortured perverse ingenuity of images which dissipates instead of concentrating the imagination, and which may be due in part to influences by which Marlowe was untouched. Next, we find that Marlowe's vice is one which he was gradually attenuating, and even, what is more miraculous, turning into a virtue. And we find that this bard of torrential imagination recognized many of his best bits (and those of one or two others), saved them, and reproduced them more than once, almost invariably improving them in the process.

It is worth while noticing a few of these versions, because they indicate, somewhat contrary to usual opinion, that Marlowe was a deliberate and conscious workman. Mr. J. G. Robertson has spotted an interesting theft of Marlowe's from Spenser. Here is Spenser (*Faery Queen*, I. vii. 32):

> Like to an almond tree y-mounted high
> > On top of green Selinis all alone,
> With blossoms brave bedeckèd daintily;
> > Whose tender locks do tremble every one
> At every little breath that under heaven is blown.

And here Marlowe (*Tamburlaine*, Part II. Act IV. sc. iii.):

> Like to an almond tree y-mounted high
> Upon the lofty and celestial mount
> Of evergreen Selinus, quaintly deck'd
> With blooms more white than Erycina's brows,
> Whose tender blossoms tremble every one
> At every little breath that thorough heaven is blown.

This is interesting, not only as showing that Marlowe's talent, like that of most poets, was partly synthetic, but also because it seems to give a clue to some particularly "lyric" effects found in *Tamburlaine*, not in Marlowe's other plays, and not, I believe, anywhere else. For example, the praise of Zenocrate in Part II. Act II. sc. iv.:

> Now walk the angels on the walls of heaven,
> As sentinels to warn th' immortal souls
> To entertain divine Zenocrate: etc.

This is not Spenser's movement, but the influence of Spenser must be present. There had been no great blank verse before Marlowe; but there was the powerful presence of this great master of melody immediately precedent; and the combination produced results which could not be repeated. I do not think that it can be claimed that Peele had any influence here.

The passage quoted from Spenser has a further interest. It will be noted that the fourth line:

> With blooms more white than Erycina's brows

is Marlowe's contribution. Compare this with these other lines of Marlowe:

> So looks my love, shadowing in her brows
> > (*Tamburlaine*)

> Like to the shadows of Pyramides
> > (*Tamburlaine*)

and the final and best version:

> Shadowing more beauty in their airy brows
> Than have the white breasts of the queen of love.
> > (*Doctor Faustus*)

and compare the whole set with Spenser again (*F. Q.*):

> Upon her eyelids many graces sate
> Under the shadow of her even brows,

a passage which Mr. Robertson says Spenser himself used in three other places.

This economy is frequent in Marlowe. Within *Tamburlaine* it occurs in the form of monotony, especially in the facile use of resonant names (*e.g.* the recurrence of "Caspia" or "Caspian" with the same tone effect), a practice in which Marlowe was followed by Milton, but which Marlowe himself outgrew. Again,

> Zenocrate, lovlier than the love of Jove,
> Brighter than is the silver Rhodope,

is paralleled later by

> Zenocrate, the lovliest maid alive,
> Fairer than rocks of pearl and precious stone.

One line Marlowe remodels with triumphant success:

> And set black streamers in the firmament
> (*Tamburlaine*)

becomes

> See, see, where Christ's blood streams in the firmament!
> (*Doctor Faustus*)

The verse accomplishments of *Tamburlaine* are notably two: Marlowe gets into blank verse the melody of Spenser, and he gets a new driving power by reinforcing the sentence period against the line period. The rapid long sentence, running line into line, as in the famous soliloquies "Nature compounded of four elements" and "What is beauty, saith my sufferings, then?" marks the certain escape of blank verse from the rhymed couplet, and from the elegiac or rather pastoral note of Surrey, to which Tennyson returned. If you contrast these two soliloquies with the verse of Marlowe's greatest contemporary, Kyd—by no means a despicable versifier—you see the importance of the innovation:

> The one took sanctuary, and, being sent for out,
> Was murdered in Southwark as he passed

> To Greenwich, where the Lord Protector lay.
> Black Will was burned in Flushing on a stage;
> Green was hanged at Osbridge in Kent . . .

which is not really inferior to:

> So these four abode
> Within one house together; and as years
> Went forward, Mary took another mate;
> But Dora lived unmarried till her death.
> (Tennyson, *Dora*)

In *Faustus* Marlowe went farther: he broke up the line, to a gain in intensity, in the last soliloquy; and he developed a new and important conversational tone in the dialogues of Faustus with the devil. *Edward II.* has never lacked consideration: it is more desirable, in brief space, to remark upon two plays, one of which has been misunderstood and the other underrated. These are the *Jew of Malta* and *Dido Queen of Carthage*. Of the first of these, it has always been said that the end, even the last two acts, are unworthy of the first three. If one takes the *Jew of Malta* not as a tragedy, or as a "tragedy of blood," but as a farce, the concluding act becomes intelligible; and if we attend with a careful ear to the versification, we find that Marlowe develops a tone to suit this farce, and even perhaps that this tone is his most powerful and mature tone. I say farce, but with the enfeebled humour of our times the word is a misnomer; it is the farce of the old English humour, the terribly serious, even savage comic humour, the humour which spent its last breath on the decadent genius of Dickens. It has nothing in common with J. M. Barrie, Captain Bairnsfather, or *Punch*. It is the humour of that very serious (but very different) play, *Volpone*.

> First, be thou void of these affections,
> Compassion, love, vain hope, and heartless fear;

> Be moved at nothing, see thou pity none . . .
> As for myself, I walk abroad o' nights,
> And kill sick people groaning under walls:
> Sometimes I go about and poison wells . . .

and the last words of Barabas complete this prodigious caricature:

> But now begins th' extremity of heat
> To pinch me with intolerable pangs:
> Die, life! fly, soul! tongue, curse thy fill, and die!

It is something which Shakespeare could not do, and which he could not have understood.

Dido appears to be a hurried play, perhaps done to order with the *Æneid* in front of him. But even here there is progress. The account of the sack of Troy is in this newer style of Marlowe's, this style which secures its emphasis by always hesitating on the edge of caricature at the right moment:

> The Grecian soldiers, tir'd with ten years war,
> Began to cry, "Let us unto our ships,
> Troy is invincible, why stay we here?" . . .
>
> But this, the camp was come unto the walls,
> And through the breach did march into the streets,
> Where, meeting with the rest, "Kill, kill!" they cried. . . .
>
> And after him, his band of Myrmidons,
> With balls of wild-fire in their murdering paws . . .
>
> At last, the soldiers pull'd her by the heels,
> And swung her howling in the empty air. . . .
>
> We saw Cassandra sprawling in the streets . . .

This is not Vergil, or Shakespeare; it is pure Marlowe. By comparing the whole speech with Clarence's dream, in

Richard III., one acquires a little insight into the difference between Marlowe and Shakespeare:

> What scourge for perjury
> Can this dark monarchy afford false Clarence?

There, on the other hand, is what Marlowe's style could not do; the phrase has a concision which is almost classical, certainly Dantesque. Again, as often with the Elizabethan dramatists, there are lines in Marlowe, besides the many lines that Shakespeare adapted, that might have been written by either:

> If thou wilt stay,
> Leap in mine arms; mine arms are open wide;
> If not, turn from me, and I'll turn from thee;
> For though thou hast the heart to say farewell,
> I have not power to stay thee.

But the direction in which Marlowe's verse might have moved, had he not "dyed swearing," is quite un-Shakespearean, is toward this intense and serious and indubitably great poetry, which, like some great painting and sculpture, attains its effects by something not unlike caricature.

HAMLET AND HIS PROBLEMS

Few critics have admitted that *Hamlet* the play is the primary problem, and Hamlet the character only secondary. And Hamlet the character has had an especial temptation for that most dangerous type of critic: the critic with a mind which is naturally of the creative order, but which through some weakness in creative power exercises itself in criticism instead. These minds often find in Hamlet a vicarious existence for their own artistic realization. Such a mind had Goethe, who made of Hamlet a Werther; and such had Coleridge, who made of Hamlet a Coleridge; and probably neither of these men in writing about Hamlet remembered that his first business was to study a work of art. The kind of criticism that Goethe and Coleridge produced, in writing of Hamlet, is the most misleading kind possible. For they both possessed unquestionable critical insight, and both make their critical aberrations the more plausible by the substitution—of their own Hamlet for Shakespeare's—which their creative gift effects. We should be thankful that Walter Pater did not fix his attention on this play.

Two recent writers, Mr. J. M. Robertson and Professor Stoll of the University of Minnesota, have issued small books which can be praised for moving in the other direction. Mr. Stoll performs a service in recalling to our attention the labours of the critics of the seventeenth and eighteenth centuries,[1] observing that

> they knew less about psychology than more recent Hamlet crit-
> ics, but they were nearer in spirit to Shakespeare's art; and as they
> insisted on the importance of the effect of the whole rather than
> on the importance of the leading character, they were nearer, in
> their old-fashioned way, to the secret of dramatic art in general.

Qua work of art, the work of art cannot be interpreted; there is nothing to interpret; we can only criticize it according to standards, in comparison to other works of art; and for "interpretation" the chief task is the presentation of relevant historical facts which the reader is not assumed to know. Mr. Robertson points out, very pertinently, how critics have failed in their "interpretation" of *Hamlet* by ignoring what ought to be very obvious: that *Hamlet* is a stratification, that it represents the efforts of a series of men, each making what he could out of the work of his predecessors. The *Hamlet* of Shakespeare will appear to us very differently if, instead of treating the whole action of the play as due to Shakespeare's design, we perceive his *Hamlet* to be superposed upon much cruder material which persists even in the final form.

We know that there was an older play by Thomas Kyd, that extraordinary dramatic (if not poetic) genius who was in all probability the author of two plays so dissimilar as the *Spanish Tragedy* and *Arden of Feversham;* and what this play was like we can guess from three clues: from the *Spanish Tragedy* itself, from the tale of Belleforest upon which Kyd's *Hamlet* must have been based, and from a version acted in Germany in Shakespeare's lifetime which bears strong evidence of having been adapted from the earlier, not the later, play. From these three sources it is clear that in the earlier play the motive was

---

[1] I have never, by the way, seen a cogent refutation of Thomas Rymer's objections to *Othello.*

a revenge-motive simply; that the action or delay is caused, as in the *Spanish Tragedy,* solely by the difficulty of assassinating a monarch surrounded by guards; and that the "madness" of Hamlet was feigned in order to escape suspicion, and successfully. In the final play of Shakespeare, on the other hand, there is a motive which is more important than that of revenge, and which explicitly "blunts" the latter; the delay in revenge is unexplained on grounds of necessity or expediency; and the effect of the "madness" is not to lull but to arouse the king's suspicion. The alteration is not complete enough, however, to be convincing. Furthermore, there are verbal parallels so close to the *Spanish Tragedy* as to leave no doubt that in places Shakespeare was merely *revising* the text of Kyd. And finally there are unexplained scenes—the Polonius-Laertes and the Polonius-Reynaldo scenes—for which there is little excuse; these scenes are not in the verse style of Kyd, and not beyond doubt in the style of Shakespeare. These Mr. Robertson believes to be scenes in the original play of Kyd reworked by a third hand, perhaps Chapman, before Shakespeare touched the play. And he concludes, with very strong show of reason, that the original play of Kyd was, like certain other revenge plays, in two parts of five acts each. The upshot of Mr. Robertson's examination is, we believe, irrefragable: that Shakespeare's *Hamlet,* so far as it is Shakespeare's, is a play dealing with the effect of a mother's guilt upon her son, and that Shakespeare was unable to impose this motive successfully upon the "intractable" material of the old play.

Of the intractability there can be no doubt. So far from being Shakespeare's masterpiece, the play is most certainly an artistic failure. In several ways the play is puzzling, and disquieting as is none of the others. Of all the plays it is the longest and is possibly the one on which Shakespeare spent most pains; and yet he has left in it superfluous and inconsistent scenes which even hasty revision should have noticed. The versification is variable. Lines like

> Look, the morn, in russet mantle clad,
> Walks o'er the dew of yon high eastern hill,

are of the Shakespeare of *Romeo and Juliet.* The lines in Act v.
sc. ii.,

> Sir, in my heart there was a kind of fighting
> That would not let me sleep . . .
> Up from my cabin,
> My sea-gown scarf'd about me, in the dark
> Grop'd I to find out them: had my desire;
> Finger'd their packet;

are of his quite mature. Both workmanship and thought are in
an unstable condition. We are surely justified in attributing
the play, with that other profoundly interesting play of "in-
tractable" material and astonishing versification, *Measure for
Measure,* to a period of crisis, after which follow the tragic suc-
cesses which culminate in *Coriolanus. Coriolanus* may be not as
"interesting" as *Hamlet,* but it is, with *Antony and Cleopatra,*
Shakespeare's most assured artistic success. And probably
more people have thought *Hamlet* a work of art because they
found it interesting, than have found it interesting because it
is a work of art. It is the "Mona Lisa" of literature.

The grounds of *Hamlet*'s failure are not immediately obvi-
ous. Mr. Robertson is undoubtedly correct in concluding
that the essential emotion of the play is the feeling of a son
towards a guilty mother:

> [Hamlet's] tone is that of one who has suffered tortures on the
> score of his mother's degradation. . . . The guilt of a mother is an
> almost intolerable motive for drama, but it had to be maintained
> and emphasized to supply a psychological solution, or rather a
> hint of one.

This, however, is by no means the whole story. It is not merely
the "guilt of a mother" that cannot be handled as Shakespeare

handled the suspicion of Othello, the infatuation of Antony, or the pride of Coriolanus. The subject might conceivably have expanded into a tragedy like these, intelligible, self-complete, in the sunlight. *Hamlet,* like the sonnets, is full of some stuff that the writer could not drag to light, contemplate, or manipulate into art. And when we search for this feeling, we find it, as in the sonnets, very difficult to localize. You cannot point to it in the speeches; indeed, if you examine the two famous soliloquies you see the versification of Shakespeare, but a content which might be claimed by another, perhaps by the author of the *Revenge of Bussy d' Ambois,* Act v. sc. i. We find Shakespeare's *Hamlet* not in the action, not in any quotations that we might select, so much as in an unmistakable tone which is unmistakably not in the earlier play.

The only way of expressing emotion in the form of art is by finding an "objective correlative"; in other words, a set of objects, a situation, a chain of events which shall be the formula of that *particular* emotion; such that when the external facts, which must terminate in sensory experience, are given, the emotion is immediately evoked. If you examine any of Shakespeare's more successful tragedies, you will find this exact equivalence; you will find that the state of mind of Lady Macbeth walking in her sleep has been communicated to you by a skilful accumulation of imagined sensory impressions; the words of Macbeth on hearing of his wife's death strike us as if, given the sequence of events, these words were automatically released by the last event in the series. The artistic "inevitability" lies in this complete adequacy of the external to the emotion; and this is precisely what is deficient in *Hamlet.* Hamlet (the man) is dominated by an emotion which is inexpressible, because it is in *excess* of the facts as they appear. And the supposed identity of Hamlet with his author is genuine to this point: that Hamlet's bafflement at the absence of objective equivalent to his feelings is a prolongation of the bafflement of his creator in the face of his artistic problem. Hamlet is up against the difficulty that his disgust is occasioned by his mother, but that his mother is not an adequate equivalent for it; his disgust envelops and exceeds her. It is thus a feeling which he cannot understand; he cannot objectify it, and it therefore remains to poison life and obstruct action. None of the possible actions can satisfy it; and nothing that Shakespeare can do with the plot can express Hamlet for him. And it must be noticed that the very nature of the *donées* of the problem precludes objective equivalence. To have heightened the criminality of Gertrude would have been to provide the formula for a totally different emotion in Hamlet; it is just *because* her character is so negative and insignificant that she arouses in Hamlet the feeling which she is incapable of representing.

The "madness" of Hamlet lay to Shakespeare's hand; in the earlier play a simple ruse, and to the end, we may presume, understood as a ruse by the audience. For Shakespeare it is less than madness and more than feigned. The levity of Hamlet, his repetition of phrase, his puns, are not part of a deliberate plan of dissimulation, but a form of emotional relief. In the character Hamlet it is the buffoonery of an emotion which can find no outlet in action; in the dramatist it is the buffoonery of an emotion which he cannot express in art. The intense feeling, ecstatic or terrible, without an object or exceeding its object, is something which every person of sensibility has known; it is doubtless a study to pathologists. It often occurs in adolescence: the ordinary person puts these feelings to sleep, or trims down his feeling to fit the business world; the artist keeps it alive by his ability to intensify the world to his emotions. The Hamlet of Laforgue is an adolescent; the Hamlet of Shakespeare is not, he has not that explanation and excuse. We must simply admit that here Shakespeare tackled a problem which proved too much for him. Why he attempted it at all is an insoluble puzzle; under compulsion of what experience he attempted to express the inexpressibly horrible, we cannot ever know. We need a great many facts in his biography; and we should like to know whether, and when, and after or at the same time as what personal experience, he read Montaigne, II. xii., *Apologie de Raimond Sebond*. We should have, finally, to know something which is by hypothesis unknowable, for we assume it to be an experience which, in the manner indicated, exceeded the facts. We should have to understand things which Shakespeare did not understand himself.

BEN JONSON

The reputation of Jonson has been of the most deadly kind that can be compelled upon the memory of a great poet. To be universally accepted; to be damned by the praise that quenches all desire to read the book; to be afflicted by the imputation of the virtues which excite the least pleasure; and to be read only by historians and antiquaries—this is the most perfect conspiracy of approval. For some generations the reputation of Jonson has been carried rather as a liability than as an asset in the balance-sheet of English literature. No critic has succeeded in making him appear pleasurable or even interesting. Swinburne's book on Jonson satisfies no curiosity and stimulates no thought. For the critical study in the "Men of Letters Series" by Mr. Gregory Smith there is a place; it satisfies curiosity, it supplies many just observations, it provides valuable matter on the neglected masques; it only fails to remodel the image of Jonson which is settled in our minds. Probably the fault lies with several generations of our poets. It is not that the value of poetry is only its value to living poets for their own work; but appreciation is akin to creation, and true enjoyment of poetry is related to the stirring of suggestion, the stimulus that a poet feels in his enjoyment of other poetry. Jonson has provided no creative stimulus for a very long time; consequently we must look back as far as

Dryden—precisely, a poetic practitioner who learned from Jonson—before we find a living criticism of Jonson's work.

Yet there are possibilities for Jonson even now. We have no difficulty in seeing what brought him to this pass; how, in contrast, not with Shakespeare, but with Marlowe, Webster, Donne, Beaumont, and Fletcher, he has been paid out with reputation instead of enjoyment. He is no less a poet than these men, but his poetry is of the surface. Poetry of the surface cannot be understood without study; for to deal with the surface of life, as Jonson dealt with it, is to deal so deliberately that we too must be deliberate, in order to understand. Shakespeare, and smaller men also, are in the end more difficult, but they offer something at the start to encourage the student or to satisfy those who want nothing more; they are suggestive, evocative, a phrase, a voice; they offer poetry in detail as well as in design. So does Dante offer something, a phrase everywhere (*tu se' ombra ed ombra vedi*) even to readers who have no Italian; and Dante and Shakespeare have poetry of design as well as of detail. But the polished veneer of Jonson reflects only the lazy reader's fatuity; unconscious does not respond to unconscious; no swarms of inarticulate feelings are aroused. The immediate appeal of Jonson is to the mind; his emotional tone is not in the single verse, but in the design of the whole. But not many people are capable of discovering for themselves the beauty which is only found after labour; and Jonson's industrious readers have been those whose interest was historical and curious, and those who have thought that in discovering the historical and curious interest they had discovered the artistic value as well. When we say that Jonson requires study, we do not mean study of his classical scholarship or of seventeenth-century manners. We mean intelligent saturation in his work as a whole; we mean that in order to enjoy him at all, we must get to the centre of his work and his temperament, and that we must see him unbiased by time, as a contemporary. And to see him as a contemporary does not so much require the power of putting ourselves into seventeenth-century London as it requires the power of setting Jonson in our London: a more difficult triumph of divination.

It is generally conceded that Jonson failed as a tragic dramatist; and it is usually agreed that he failed because his genius was for satiric comedy and because of the weight of pedantic learning with which he burdened his two tragic failures. The second point marks an obvious error of detail; the first is too crude a statement to be accepted; to say that he failed because his genius was unsuited to tragedy is to tell us nothing at all. Jonson did not write a good tragedy, but we can see no reason why he should not have written one. If two plays so different as *The Tempest* and *The Silent Woman* are both comedies, surely the category of tragedy could be made wide enough to include something possible for Jonson to have done. But the classification of tragedy and comedy, while it may be sufficient to mark the distinction in a dramatic literature of more rigid form and treatment—it may distinguish Aristophanes from Euripides—is not adequate to a drama of such variations as the Elizabethans. Tragedy is a crude classification for plays so different in their tone as *Macbeth, The Jew of Malta,* and *The Witch of Edmonton;* and it does not help us much to say that *The Merchant of Venice* and *The Alchemist* are comedies. Jonson had his own scale, his own instrument. The merit which *Catiline* possesses is the same merit that is exhibited more triumphantly in *Volpone; Catiline* fails, not because it is too laboured and conscious, but because it is not conscious enough; because Jonson in this play was not alert to his own idiom, not clear in his mind as to what his temperament wanted him to do. In *Catiline* Jonson conforms, or attempts to conform, to conventions; not to the conventions of antiquity, which he had exquisitely under control, but to the conventions of tragico-historical drama of his time. It is not the Latin erudition that sinks *Catiline,* but the application of that erudition to a form which was not the proper vehicle for the mind which had amassed the erudition.

If you look at *Catiline*—that dreary Pyrrhic victory of
tragedy—you find two passages to be successful: Act ii. scene
I, the dialogue of the political ladies, and the Prologue of
Sylla's ghost. These two passages are genial. The soliloquy of
the ghost is a characteristic Jonson success in content and in
versification—

> Dost thou not feel me, Rome? not yet! is night
> So heavy on thee, and my weight so light?
> Can Sylla's ghost arise within thy walls,
> Less threatening than an earthquake, the quick falls
> Of thee and thine? Shake not the frighted heads
> Of thy steep towers, or shrink to their first beds?
> Or as their ruin the large Tyber fills,
> Make that swell up, and drown thy seven proud hills? . . .

This is the learned, but also the creative, Jonson. Without
concerning himself with the character of Sulla, and in lines of
invective, Jonson makes Sylla's ghost, while the words are
spoken, a living and terrible force. The words fall with as de-
termined beat as if they were the will of the morose Dictator
himself. You may say: merely invective; but mere invective,
even if as superior to the clumsy fisticuffs of Marston and
Hall as Jonson's verse is superior to theirs, would not create a
living figure as Jonson has done in this long tirade. And you
may say: rhetoric; but if we are to call it "rhetoric" we must
subject that term to a closer dissection than any to which it is
accustomed. What Jonson has done here is not merely a fine
speech. It is the careful, precise filling in of a strong and sim-
ple outline, and at no point does it overflow the outline; it is
far more careful and precise in its obedience to this outline
than are many of the speeches in *Tamburlaine*. The outline is
not Sulla, for Sulla has nothing to do with it, but "Sylla's
ghost." The words may not be suitable to an historical Sulla,
or to anybody in history, but they are a perfect expression for
"Sylla's ghost." You cannot say they are rhetorical "because

people do not talk like that," you cannot call them "verbiage"; they do not exhibit prolixity or redundancy or the other vices in the rhetoric books; there is a definite artistic emotion which demands expression at that length. The words themselves are mostly simple words, the syntax is natural, the language austere rather than adorned. Turning then to the induction of *The Poetaster*, we find another success of the same kind—

> Light, I salute thee, but with wounded nerves . . .

Men may not talk in that way, but the spirit of envy does, and in the words of Jonson envy is a real and living person. It is not human life that informs envy and Sylla's ghost, but it is energy of which human life is only another variety.

Returning to *Catiline*, we find that the best scene in the body of the play is one which cannot be squeezed into a tragic frame, and which appears to belong to satiric comedy. The scene between Fulvia and Galla and Sempronia is a living scene in a wilderness of oratory. And as it recalls other scenes—there is a suggestion of the college of ladies in *The Silent Woman*—it looks like a comedy scene. And it appears to be satire.

> They shall all give and pay well, that come here,
> If they will have it; and that, jewels, pearl,
> Plate, or round sums to buy these. I'm not taken
> With a cob-swan or a high-mounting bull,
> As foolish Leda and Europa were;
> But the bright gold, with Danaë. For such price
> I would endure a rough, harsh Jupiter,
> Or ten such thundering gamesters, and refrain
> To laugh at 'em, till they are gone, with my much suffering.

This scene is no more comedy than it is tragedy, and the "satire" is merely a medium for the essential emotion. Jonson's drama is only incidentally satire, because it is only incidentally a criticism upon the actual world. It is not satire in the way in which the work of Swift or the work of Molière may be called satire: that is, it does not find its source in any precise emotional attitude or precise intellectual criticism of the actual world. It is satire perhaps as the work of Rabelais is satire; certainly not more so. The important thing is that if fiction can be divided into creative fiction and critical fiction, Jonson's is creative. That he was a great critic, our first great critic, does not affect this assertion. Every creator is also a critic; Jonson was a conscious critic, but he was also conscious in his creations. Certainly, one sense in which the term "critical" may be applied to fiction is a sense in which the term might be used of a method antithetical to Jonson's. It is the method of *Education Sentimentale.* The characters of Jonson, of Shakespeare, perhaps of all the greatest drama, are drawn in positive and simple outlines. They may be filled in, and by Shakespeare they are filled in, by much detail or many shifting aspects; but a clear and sharp and simple form remains through these—though it would be hard to say in what the clarity and sharpness and simplicity of Hamlet consists. But Frédéric Moreau is not made in that way. He is constructed partly by negative definition, built up by a great number of observations. We cannot isolate him from the environment in which we find him; it may be an environment which is or can be much universalized; nevertheless it, and the figure in it, consist of very many observed particular facts, the actual world. Without this world the figure dissolves. The ruling faculty is a critical perception, a commentary upon experienced feeling and sensation. If this is true of Flaubert, it is true in a higher degree of Molière than of Jonson. The broad farcical lines of Molière may seem to be the same drawing as Jonson's. But Molière—say in Alceste or Monsieur Jourdain—is criticizing the actual; the reference to the actual world is more direct. And having a more tenuous reference, the work of Jonson is much less directly satirical.

This leads us to the question of Humours. Largely on the

evidence of the two Humour plays, it is sometimes assumed that Jonson is occupied with types; typical exaggerations, or exaggerations of type. The Humour definition, the expressed intention of Jonson, may be satisfactory for these two plays. *Every Man in his Humour* is the first mature work of Jonson, and the student of Jonson must study it; but it is not the play in which Jonson found his genius: it is the last of his plays to read first. If one reads *Volpone,* and after that re-reads the *Jew of Malta;* then returns to Jonson and reads *Bartholomew Fair, The Alchemist, Epicœne* and *The Devil is an Ass,* and finally *Catiline,* it is possible to arrive at a fair opinion of the poet and the dramatist.

The Humour, even at the beginning, is not a type, as in Marston's satire, but a simplified and somewhat distorted individual with a typical mania. In the later work, the Humour definition quite fails to account for the total effect produced. The characters of Shakespeare are such as might exist in different circumstances than those in which Shakespeare sets them. The latter appear to be those which extract from the characters the most intense and interesting realization; but that realization has not exhausted their possibilities. Volpone's life, on the other hand, is bounded by the scene in which it is played; in fact, the life is the life of the scene and is derivatively the life of Volpone; the life of the character is inseparable from the life of the drama. This is not dependence upon a background, or upon a substratum of fact. The emotional effect is single and simple. Whereas in Shakespeare the effect is due to the way in which the characters *act upon* one another, in Jonson it is given by the way in which the characters *fit in* with each other. The artistic result of *Volpone* is not due to any effect that Volpone, Mosca, Corvino, Corbaccio, Voltore have upon each other, but simply to their combination into a whole. And these figures are not personifications of passions; separately, they have not even that reality, they are constituents. It is a similar indication of Jonson's method that you can hardly pick out a line of Jonson's and say confidently that it is great poetry; but there are many extended passages to which you cannot deny that honour.

> I will have all my beds blown up, not stuft;
> Down is too hard; and then, mine oval room
> Fill'd with such pictures as Tiberius took
> From Elephantis, and dull Aretine
> But coldly imitated. Then, my glasses
> Cut in more subtle angles, to disperse
> And multiply the figures, as I walk....

Jonson is the legitimate heir of Marlowe. The man who wrote, in *Volpone:*

> for thy love,
> In varying figures, I would have contended
> With the blue Proteus, or the hornèd flood....

and

> See, a carbuncle
> May put out both the eyes of our Saint Mark;
> A diamond would have bought Lollia Paulina,
> When she came in like star-light, hid with jewels....

is related to Marlowe as a poet; and if Marlowe is a poet, Jonson is also. And, if Jonson's comedy is a comedy of humours, then Marlowe's tragedy, a large part of it, is a tragedy of humours. But Jonson has too exclusively been considered as the typical representative of a point of view toward comedy. He has suffered from his great reputation as a critic and theorist, from the effects of his intelligence. We have been taught to think of him as the man, the dictator (confusedly in our minds with his later namesake), as the literary politician impressing his views upon a generation; we are offended by the constant reminder of his scholarship. We forget the comedy in the humours, and the serious artist in the scholar. Jonson has suffered in public opinion, as anyone must suffer who is forced to talk about his art.

If you examine the first hundred lines or more of *Volpone* the verse appears to be in the manner of Marlowe, more deliberate, more mature, but without Marlowe's inspiration. It looks like mere "rhetoric," certainly not "deeds and language such as men do use"! It appears to us, in fact, forced and flagitious bombast. That it is not "rhetoric," or at least not vicious rhetoric, we do not know until we are able to review the whole play. For the consistent maintenance of this manner conveys in the end an effect not of verbosity, but of bold, even shocking and terrifying directness. We have difficulty in saying exactly what produces this simple and single effect. It is not in any ordinary way due to management of intrigue. Jonson employs immense dramatic constructive skill: it is not so much skill in plot as skill in doing without a plot. He never manipulates as complicated a plot as that of *The Merchant of Venice;* he has in his best plays nothing like the intrigue of Restoration comedy. In *Bartholomew Fair* it is hardly a plot at all; the marvel of the play is the bewildering rapid chaotic action of the fair; it is the fair itself, not anything that happens to take place in the fair. In *Volpone,* or *The Alchemist,* or *The Silent Woman,* the plot is enough to keep the players in motion; it is rather an "action" than a plot. The plot does not hold the play together; what holds the play together is a unity of inspiration that radiates into plot and personages alike.

We have attempted to make more precise the sense in which it was said that Jonson's work is "of the surface"; carefully avoiding the word "superficial." For there is work contemporary with Jonson's which is superficial in a pejorative sense in which the word cannot be applied to Jonson—the work of Beaumont and Fletcher. If we look at the work of Jonson's great contemporaries, Shakespeare, and also Donne and Webster and Tourneur (and sometimes Middleton), have a depth, a third dimension, as Mr. Gregory Smith rightly calls it, which Jonson's work has not. Their words have often a network of tentacular roots reaching down to the deepest terrors and desires. Jonson's most certainly have not; but in Beaumont and Fletcher we may think that at times we find it. Looking closer, we discover that the blossoms of Beaumont and Fletcher's imagination draw no sustenance from the soil, but are cut and slightly withered flowers stuck into sand.

> Wilt thou, hereafter, when they talk of me,
> As thou shalt hear nothing but infamy,
> Remember some of these things? . . .
> I pray thee, do; for thou shalt never see me so again.

> Hair woven in many a curious warp,
> Able in endless error to enfold
> The wandering soul; . . .

Detached from its context, this looks like the verse of the greater poets; just as lines of Jonson, detached from their context, look like inflated or empty fustian. But the evocative quality of the verse of Beaumont and Fletcher depends upon a clever appeal to emotions and associations which they have not themselves grasped; it is hollow. It is superficial with a vacuum behind it; the superficies of Jonson is solid. It is what it is; it does not pretend to be another thing. But it is so very conscious and deliberate that we must look with eyes alert to the whole before we apprehend the significance of any part. We cannot call a man's work superficial when it is the creation of a world; a man cannot be accused of dealing superficially with the world which he himself has created; the superficies *is* the world. Jonson's characters conform to the logic of the emotions of their world. It is a world like Lobatchevsky's; the worlds created by artists like Jonson are like systems of non-Euclidean geometry. They are not fancy, because they have a logic of their own; and this logic illuminates the actual world, because it gives us a new point of view from which to inspect it.

A writer of power and intelligence, Jonson endeavoured to promulgate, as a formula and programme of reform, what he chose to do himself; and he not unnaturally laid down in abstract theory what is in reality a personal point of view. And it is in the end of no value to discuss Jonson's theory and practice unless we recognize and seize this point of view, which escapes the formulæ, and which is what makes his plays worth reading. Jonson behaved as the great creative mind that he was: he created his own world, a world from which his followers, as well as the dramatists who were trying to do something wholly different, are excluded. Remembering this, we turn to Mr. Gregory Smith's objection—that Jonson's characters lack the third dimension, have no life out of the theatrical existence in which they appear—and demand an inquest. The objection implies that the characters are purely the work of intellect, or the result of superficial observation of a world which is faded or mildewed. It implies that the characters are lifeless. But if we dig beneath the theory, beneath the observation, beneath the deliberate drawing and the theatrical and dramatic elaboration, there is discovered a kind of power, animating Volpone, Busy, Fitzdottrel, the literary ladies of *Epicœne*, even Bobadil, which comes from below the intellect, and for which no theory of humours will account. And it is the same kind of power which vivifies Trimalchio, and Panurge, and some but not all of the "comic" characters of Dickens. The fictive life of this kind is not to be circumscribed by a reference to "comedy" or to "farce"; it is not exactly the kind of life which informs the characters of Molière or that which informs those of Marivaux—two writers who were, besides, doing something quite different the one from the other. But it is something which distinguishes Barabas from Shylock, Epicure Mammon from Falstaff, Faustus from—if you will—Macbeth; Marlowe and Jonson from Shakespeare and the Shakespearians, Webster, and Tourneur. It is not merely Humours: for neither Volpone nor Mosca is a humour. No theory of humours could account for Jonson's best plays or the best characters in them. We want to know at what point the comedy of humours passes into a work of art, and why Jonson is not Brome.

The creation of a work of art, we will say the creation of a character in a drama, consists in the process of transfusion of the personality, or, in a deeper sense, the life, of the author into the character. This is a very different matter from the orthodox creation in one's own image. The ways in which the passions and desires of the creator may be satisfied in the work of art are complex and devious. In a painter they may take the form of a predilection for certain colours, tones, or lightings; in a writer the original impulse may be even more strangely transmuted. Now, we may say with Mr. Gregory Smith that Falstaff or a score of Shakespeare's characters have a "third dimension" that Jonson's have not. This will mean, not that Shakespeare's spring from the feelings or imagination and Jonson's from the intellect or invention; they have equally an emotional source; but that Shakespeare's represent a more complex tissue of feelings and desires, as well as a more supple, a more susceptible temperament. Falstaff is not only the roast Malmesbury ox with the pudding in his belly; he also "grows old," and, finally, his nose is as sharp as a pen. He was perhaps the *satisfaction* of more, and of more complicated feelings; and perhaps he was, as the great tragic characters must have been, the offspring of deeper, less apprehensible feelings: deeper, but not necessarily stronger or more intense, than those of Jonson. It is obvious that the spring of the difference is not the difference between feeling and thought, or superior insight, superior perception, on the part of Shakespeare, but his susceptibility to a greater range of emotion, and emotion deeper and more obscure. But his characters are no more "alive" than are the characters of Jonson.

The world they live in is a larger one. But small worlds—the worlds which artists create—do not differ only in magnitude; if they are complete worlds, drawn to scale in every part, they differ in kind also. And Jonson's world has this scale.

His type of personality found its relief in something falling under the category of burlesque or farce—though when you are dealing with a *unique* world, like his, these terms fail to appease the desire for definition. It is not, at all events, the farce of Molière: the latter is more analytic, more an intellectual redistribution. It is not defined by the word "satire." Jonson poses as a satirist. But satire like Jonson's is great in the end not by hitting off its object, but by creating it; the satire is merely the means which leads to the æsthetic result, the impulse which projects a new world into a new orbit. In *Every Man in his Humour* there is a neat, a very neat, comedy of humours. In discovering and proclaiming in this play the new genre Jonson was simply recognizing, unconsciously, the route which opened out in the proper direction for his instincts. His characters are and remain, like Marlowe's, simplified characters; but the simplification does not consist in the dominance of a particular humour or monomania. That is a very superficial account of it. The simplification consists largely in reduction of detail, in the seizing of aspects relevant to the relief of an emotional impulse which remains the same for that character, in making the character conform to a particular setting. This stripping is essential to the art, to which is also essential a flat distortion in the drawing; it is an art of caricature, of great caricature, like Marlowe's. It is a great caricature, which is beautiful; and a great humour, which is serious. The "world" of Jonson is sufficiently large; it is a world of poetic imagination; it is sombre. He did not get the third dimension, but he was not trying to get it.

If we approach Jonson with less frozen awe of his learning, with a clearer understanding of his "rhetoric" and its applications, if we grasp the fact that the knowledge required of the reader is not archæology but knowledge of Jonson, we can derive not only instruction in non-Euclidean humanity—but enjoyment. We can even apply him, be aware of him as a part of our literary inheritance craving further expression. Of all the dramatists of his time, Jonson is probably the one whom the present age would find the most sympathetic, if it knew him. There is a brutality, a lack of sentiment, a polished surface, a handling of large bold designs in brilliant colours, which ought to attract about three thousand people in London and elsewhere. At least, if we had a contemporary Shakespeare and a contemporary Jonson, it would be the Jonson who would arouse the enthusiasm of the intelligentsia! Though he is saturated in literature, he never sacrifices the theatrical qualities—theatrical in the most favourable sense—to literature or to the study of character. His work is a titanic show. But Jonson's masques, an important part of his work, are neglected; our flaccid culture lets shows and literature fade, but prefers faded literature to faded shows. There are hundreds of people who have read *Comus* to ten who have read the *Masque of Blackness. Comus* contains fine poetry, and poetry exemplifying some merits to which Jonson's masque poetry cannot pretend. Nevertheless, *Comus* is the death of the masque; it is the transition of a form of art—even of a form which existed for but a short generation—into "literature," literature cast in a form which has lost its application. Even though *Comus* was a masque at Ludlow Castle, Jonson had, what Milton came perhaps too late to have, a sense for living art; his art was applied. The masques can still be read, and with pleasure, by anyone who will take the trouble—a trouble which in this part of Jonson is, indeed, a study of antiquities—to imagine them in action, displayed with the music, costume, dances, and the scenery of Inigo Jones. They are additional evidence that Jonson had a fine sense of form, of the purpose for which a particular form is intended; evidence that he was a literary artist even more than he was a man of letters.

PHILIP MASSINGER

I

Massinger has been more fortunately and more fairly judged than several of his greater contemporaries. Three critics have done their best by him: the notes of Coleridge exemplify Coleridge's fragmentary and fine perceptions; the essay of Leslie Stephen is a piece of formidable destructive analysis; and the essay of Swinburne is Swinburne's criticism at its best. None of these, probably, has put Massinger finally and irrefutably into a place.

English criticism is inclined to argue or persuade rather than to state; and, instead of forcing the subject to expose himself, these critics have left in their work an undissolved residuum of their own good taste, which, however impeccable, is something that requires our faith. The principles which animate this taste remain unexplained. Mr. Cruickshank's book is a work of scholarship; and the advantage of good scholarship is that it presents us with evidence which is an invitation to the critical faculty of the reader: it bestows a method, rather than a judgment.

It is difficult—it is perhaps the supreme difficulty of criticism—to make the facts generalize themselves; but Mr. Cruickshank at least presents us with facts which are capable of generalization. This is a service of value; and it is therefore wholly a compliment to the author to say that his appendices are as valuable as the essay itself.

The sort of labour to which Mr. Cruickshank has devoted himself is one that professed critics ought more willingly to undertake. It is an important part of criticism, more important than any mere expression of opinion. To understand Elizabethan drama it is necessary to study a dozen playwrights at once, to dissect with all care the complex growth, to ponder collaboration to the utmost line. Reading Shakespeare and several of his contemporaries is pleasure enough, perhaps all the pleasure possible, for most. But if we wish to consummate and refine this pleasure by understanding it, to distill the last drop of it, to press and press the essence of each author, to apply exact measurement to our own sensations, then we must compare; and we cannot compare without parcelling the threads of authorship and influence. We must employ Mr. Cruickshank's method to examine Mr. Cruickshank's judgments; and perhaps the most important judgment to which he has committed himself is this:—

> Massinger, in his grasp of stagecraft, his flexible metre, his desire in the sphere of ethics to exploit both vice and virtue, is typical of an age which had much culture, but which, without being exactly corrupt, lacked moral fibre.

Here, in fact, is our text: to elucidate this sentence would be to account for Massinger. We begin vaguely with good taste, by a recognition that Massinger is inferior: can we trace this inferiority, dissolve it, and have left any element of merit?

We turn first to the parallel quotations from Massinger and Shakespeare collocated by Mr. Cruickshank to make manifest Massinger's indebtedness. One of the surest of tests is the way in which a poet borrows. Immature poets imitate; mature poets steal; bad poets deface what they take, and good poets make it into something better, or at least something different. The good poet welds his theft into a whole of feeling which is unique, utterly different from that from which it was torn; the bad poet throws it into something which has no cohesion. A good poet will usually borrow from authors remote in time, or alien in language, or diverse in interest. Chapman borrowed from Seneca; Shakespeare and Webster from Montaigne. The two great followers of Shakespeare, Webster and Tourneur, in their mature work do not borrow from him; he is too close to them to be of use to them in this way. Massinger, as Mr. Cruickshank shows, borrows from Shakespeare a good deal. Let us profit by some of the quotations with which he has provided us—

Massinger: Can I call back yesterday, with all their aids
            That bow unto my sceptre? or restore
            My mind to that tranquillity and peace
            It then enjoyed?

Shakespeare: Not poppy, nor mandragora,
            Nor all the drowsy syrops of the world
            Shall ever medecine thee to that sweet sleep
            Which thou owedst yesterday.

Massinger's is a general rhetorical question, the language just and pure, but colourless. Shakespeare's has particular significance; and the adjective "drowsy" and the verb "medecine" infuse a precise vigour. This is, on Massinger's part, an echo rather than an imitation or a plagiarism—the basest, because least conscious form of borrowing. "Drowsy syrop" is a condensation of meaning frequent in Shakespeare, but rare in Massinger.

Massinger: Thou didst not borrow of Vice her indirect,
            Crooked, and abject means.

Shakespeare: God knows, my son,
            By what by-paths and indirect crook'd ways
            I met this crown.

Here, again, Massinger gives the general forensic statement, Shakespeare the particular image. "Indirect crook'd" is forceful in Shakespeare; a mere pleonasm in Massinger. "Crook'd ways" is a metaphor; Massinger's phrase only the ghost of a metaphor.

> *Massinger:* And now, in the evening,
> When thou should'st pass with honour to thy
> rest,
> Wilt thou fall like a meteor?

> *Shakespeare:* I shall fall
> Like a bright exhalation in the evening,
> And no man see me more.

Here the lines of Massinger have their own beauty. Still, a "bright exhalation" appears to the eye and makes us catch our breath in the evening; "meteor" is a dim simile; the word is worn.

> *Massinger:* What you deliver to me shall be lock'd up
> In a strong cabinet, of which you yourself
> Shall keep the key.

> *Shakespeare:* 'Tis in my memory locked,
> And you yourself shall keep the key of it.

In the preceding passage Massinger had squeezed his simile to death, here he drags it round the city at his heels; and how swift Shakespeare's figure is! We may add two more passages, not given by our commentator; here the model is Webster. They occur on the same page, an artless confession.

> Here he comes,
> His nose held up; he hath something in the wind,

is hardly comparable to "the Cardinal lifts up his nose like a foul porpoise before a storm," and when we come upon

> as tann'd galley-slaves
> Pay such as do redeem them from the oar

it is unnecessary to turn up the great lines in the *Duchess of Malfi*. Massinger fancied this galley-slave; for he comes with his oar again in the *Bondsman*—

> Never did galley-slave shake off his chains,
> Or looked on his redemption from the oar. . . .

Now these are mature plays; and the *Roman Actor* (from which we have drawn the two previous extracts) is said to have been the preferred play of its author.

We may conclude directly from these quotations that Massinger's feeling for language had outstripped his feeling for things; that his eye and his vocabulary were not in close co-operation. One of the greatest distinctions of several of his elder contemporaries—we name Middleton, Webster, Tourneur—is a gift for combining, for fusing into a single phrase, two or more diverse impressions.

> . . . . in her strong toil of grace

of Shakespeare is such a fusion; the metaphor identifies itself with what suggests it; the resultant is one and is unique—

> Does the silk worm *expend* her *yellow labours?* . . .
> Why does yon fellow *falsify highways*
> And lays his life between the judge's lips
> To *refine* such a one? keeps horse and men
> To *beat their valours* for her?

> Let the common sewer take it from distinction. . . .
> Lust and forgetfulness have been amongst us. . . .

These lines of Tourneur and of Middleton exhibit that perpetual slight alteration of language, words perpetually juxtaposed in new and sudden combinations, meanings perpetually *eingeschachtelt* into meanings, which evidences a very high development of the senses, a development of the English language which we have perhaps never equalled. And, indeed, with the end of Chapman, Middleton, Webster, Tourneur, Donne we end a period when the intellect was immediately at the tips of the senses. Sensation became word and the word was sensation. The next period is the period of Milton (though still with a Marvell in it); and this period is initiated by Massinger.

It is not that the word becomes less exact. Massinger is, in a wholly eulogistic sense, choice and correct. And the decay of the senses is not inconsistent with a greater sophistication of language. But every vital development in language is a development of feeling as well. The verse of Shakespeare and the major Shakespearian dramatists is an innovation of this kind, a true mutation of species. The verse practised by Massinger is a different verse from that of his predecessors; but it is not a development based on, or resulting from, a new way of feeling. On the contrary, it seems to lead us away from feeling altogether.

We mean that Massinger must be placed as much at the beginning of one period as at the end of another. A certain Boyle, quoted by Mr. Cruickshank, says that Milton's blank verse owes much to the study of Massinger's.

> In the indefinable touches which make up the music of a verse [says Boyle], in the artistic distribution of pauses, and in the unerring choice and grouping of just those words which strike the ear as the perfection of harmony, there are, if we leave Cyril Tourneur's *Atheist's Tragedy* out of the question, only two masters in the drama, Shakespeare in his latest period and Massinger.

This Boyle must have had a singular ear to have preferred Tourneur's apprentice work to his *Revenger's Tragedy,* and one must think that he had never glanced at Ford. But though the appraisal be ludicrous, the praise is not undeserved. Mr. Cruickshank has given us an excellent example of Massinger's syntax—

> What though my father
> Writ man before he was so, and confirm'd it,
> By numbering that day no part of his life
> In which he did not service to his country;
> Was he to be free therefore from the laws
> And ceremonious form in your decrees?
> Or else because he did as much as man
> In those three memorable overthrows,
> At Granson, Morat, Nancy, where his master,
> The warlike Charalois, with whose misfortunes
> I bear his name, lost treasure, men, and life,
> To be excused from payment of those sums
> Which (his own patrimony spent) his zeal
> To serve his country forced him to take up!

It is impossible to deny the masterly construction of this passage; perhaps there is not one living poet who could do the like. It is impossible to deny the originality. The language is pure and correct, free from muddiness or turbidity. Massinger does not confuse metaphors, or heap them one upon another. He is lucid, though not easy. But if Massinger's age, "without being exactly corrupt, lacks moral fibre," Massinger's verse, without being exactly corrupt, suffers from cerebral anæmia. To say that an involved style is necessarily a bad style would be preposterous. But such a style should follow the involutions of a mode of perceiving, registering, and digesting impressions which is also involved. It is to be feared that the feeling of Massinger is simple and overlaid with received ideas. Had Massinger had a nervous system as refined as that of Middleton, Tourneur, Webster, or Ford, his style would be a triumph. But such a nature was not at hand, and Massinger precedes, not another Shakespeare, but Milton.

Massinger is, in fact, at a further remove from Shakespeare than that other precursor of Milton—John Fletcher. Fletcher was above all an opportunist, in his verse, in his momentary effects, never quite a pastiche; in his structure ready to sacrifice everything to the single scene. To Fletcher, because he was more intelligent, less will be forgiven. Fletcher had a cunning guess at feelings, and betrayed them; Massinger was unconscious and innocent. As an artisan of the theatre he is not inferior to Fletcher, and his best tragedies have an honester unity than *Bonduca*. But the unity is superficial. In the *Roman Actor* the development of parts is out of all proportion to the central theme; in the *Unnatural Combat,* in spite of the deft handling of suspense and the quick shift from climax to a new suspense, the first part of the play is the hatred of Malefort for his son and the second part is his passion for his daughter. It is theatrical skill, not an artistic conscience arranging emotions, that holds the two parts together. In the *Duke of Milan* the appearance of Sforza at the Court of his conqueror only delays the action, or rather breaks the emotional rhythm. And we have named three of Massinger's best.

A dramatist who so skillfully welds together parts which have no reason for being together, who fabricates plays so well knit and so remote from unity, we should expect to exhibit the same synthetic cunning in character. Mr. Cruickshank, Coleridge, and Leslie Stephen are pretty well agreed that Massinger is no master of characterization. You can, in fact, put together heterogeneous parts to form a lively play; but a character, to be living, must be conceived from some emotional unity. A character is not to be composed of scattered observations of human nature, but of parts which are felt together. Hence it is that although Massinger's failure to draw a moving character is no greater than his failure to make a whole play, and probably springs from the same defective sensitiveness, yet the failure in character is more conspicuous and more disastrous. A "living" character is not necessarily "true to life." It is a person whom we can see and hear, whether he be true or false to human nature as we know it. What the creator of character needs is not so much knowledge of motives as keen sensibility; the dramatist need not understand people; but he must be exceptionally aware of them. This awareness was not given to Massinger. He inherits the traditions of conduct, female chastity, hymeneal sanctity, the fashion of honour, without either criticizing or informing them from his own experience. In the earlier drama these conventions are merely a framework, or an alloy necessary for working the metal; the metal itself consisted of unique emotions resulting inevitably from the circumstances, resulting or inhering as inevitably as the properties of a chemical compound. Middleton's heroine, for instance, in the *Changeling*, exclaims in the well-known words—

> Why, 'tis impossible thou canst be so wicked,
> To shelter such a cunning cruelty
> To make his death the murderer of my honour!

The word "honour" in such a situation is out of date, but the emotion of Beatrice at that moment, given the conditions, is as permanent and substantial as anything in human nature. The emotion of Othello in Act v. is the emotion of a man who discovers that the worst part of his own soul has been exploited by some one more clever than he; it is this emotion carried by the writer to a very high degree of intensity. Even in so late and so decayed a drama as that of Ford, the framework of emotions and morals of the time is only the vehicle for statements of feeling which are unique and imperishable: Ford's and Ford's only.

What may be considered corrupt or decadent in the morals of Massinger is not an alteration or diminution in morals; it is simply the disappearance of all the personal and real emotions which this morality supported and into which it introduced a kind of order. As soon as the emotions disappear the morality which ordered it appears hideous. Puritanism itself became repulsive only when it appeared as the survival of a restraint after the feelings which it restrained had gone. When Massinger's ladies resist temptation they do not appear to undergo any important emotion; they merely know what is expected of them; they manifest themselves to us as lubricious prudes. Any age has its conventions; and any age might appear absurd when its conventions get into the hands of a man like Massinger—a man, we mean, of so exceptionally superior a literary talent as Massinger's, and so paltry an imagination. The Elizabethan morality was an important convention; important because it was not consciously of one social class alone, because it provided a framework for emotions to which all classes could respond, and it hindered no feeling. It was not hypocritical, and it did not suppress; its dark corners are haunted by the ghosts of Mary Fitton and perhaps greater. It is a subject which has not been sufficiently investigated. Fletcher and Massinger rendered it ridiculous; not by not believing in it, but because they were men of great talents who could not vivify it; because they could not fit into it passionate, complete human characters.

The tragedy of Massinger is interesting chiefly according to the definition given before; the highest degree of verbal excellence compatible with the most rudimentary development of the senses. Massinger succeeds better in something which is not tragedy; in the romantic comedy. *A Very Woman* deserves all the praise that Swinburne, with his almost unerring gift for selection, has bestowed upon it. The probable collaboration of Fletcher had the happiest result; for certainly that admirable comic personage, the tipsy Borachia, is handled with more humour than we expect of Massinger. It is a play which would be enjoyable on the stage. The form, however, of romantic comedy is itself inferior and decadent. There is an inflexibility about the poetic drama which is by no means a matter of classical, or neoclassical, or pseudo-classical law. The poetic drama might develop forms highly different from those of Greece or England, India or Japan. Conceded the utmost freedom, the romantic drama would yet remain inferior. The poetic drama must have an emotional unity, let the emotion be whatever you like. It must have a dominant tone; and if this be strong enough, the most heterogeneous emotions may be made to reinforce it. The romantic comedy is a skilful concoction of inconsistent emotion, a *revue* of emotion. *A Very Woman* is surpassingly well plotted. The debility of romantic drama does not depend upon extravagant setting, or preposterous events, or inconceivable coincidences; all these might be found in a serious tragedy or comedy. It consists in an internal incoherence of feelings, a concatenation of emotions which signifies nothing.

From this type of play, so eloquent of emotional disorder, there was no swing back of the pendulum. Changes never come by a simple reinfusion into the form which the life has just left. The romantic drama was not a new form. Massinger dealt not with emotions so much as with the social abstractions of emotions, more generalized and therefore more quickly and easily interchangeable within the confines of a single action. He was not guided by direct communications through the nerves. Romantic drama tended, accordingly, toward what is sometimes called the "typical," but which is not the truly typical; for the *typical* figure in a drama is always particularized—an individual. The tendency of the romantic drama was toward a form which continued it in removing its more conspicuous vices, was toward a more severe external order. This form was the Heroic Drama. We look into Dryden's "Essay on Heroic Plays," and we find that "love and valour ought to be the subject of an heroic poem." Massinger, in his destruction of the old drama, had prepared the way for Dryden. The intellect had perhaps exhausted the old conventions. It was not able to supply the impoverishment of feeling.

Such are the reflections aroused by an examination of some of Massinger's plays in the light of Mr. Cruickshank's statement that Massinger's age "had much culture, but, without being exactly corrupt, lacked moral fibre." The statement may be supported. In order to fit into our estimate of Massinger the two admirable comedies—*A New Way to Pay Old Debts* and *The City Madam*—a more extensive research would be required than is possible within our limits.

II

Massinger's tragedy may be summarized for the unprepared reader as being very dreary. It is dreary, unless one is prepared by a somewhat extensive knowledge of his livelier contemporaries to grasp without fatigue precisely the elements in it which are capable of giving pleasure; or unless one is incited by a curious interest in versification. In comedy, however, Massinger was one of the few masters in the language. He was a master in a comedy which is serious, even sombre; and in one aspect of it there are only two names to mention with his: those of Marlowe and Jonson. In comedy, as a matter of fact, a greater variety of methods were discovered and employed than in tragedy. The method of Kyd, as developed by Shakespeare, was the standard for English tragedy down to Otway and to Shelley. But both individual temperament, and varying epochs, made more play with comedy. The comedy of Lyly is one thing; that of Shakespeare, followed by Beaumont and Fletcher, is another; and that of Middleton is a third. And Massinger, while he has his own comedy, is nearer to Marlowe and Jonson than to any of these.

Massinger was, in fact, as a comic writer, fortunate in the moment at which he wrote. His comedy is transitional; but it happens to be one of those transitions which contain some merit not anticipated by predecessors or refined upon by later writers. The comedy of Jonson is nearer to caricature; that of Middleton a more photographic delineation of low life. Massinger is nearer to Restoration comedy, and more like his contemporary, Shirley, in assuming a certain social level, certain distinctions of class, as a postulate of his comedy. This resemblance to later comedy is also the important point of difference between Massinger and earlier comedy. But Massinger's comedy differs just as widely from the comedy of manners proper; he is closer to that in his romantic drama— in *A Very Woman*—than in *A New Way to Pay Old Debts;* in his comedy his interest is not in the follies of love-making or the absurdities of social pretence, but in the unmasking of villainy. Just as the Old Comedy of Molière differs in principle from the New Comedy of Marivaux, so the Old Comedy of Massinger differs from the New Comedy of his contemporary Shirley. And as in France, so in England, the more farcical comedy was the more serious. Massinger's great comic rogues, Sir Giles Overreach and Luke Frugal, are members of the large English family which includes Barabas and Sir Epicure Mammon, and from which Sir Tunbelly Clumsy claims descent.

What distinguishes Massinger from Marlowe and Jonson is in the main an inferiority. The greatest comic characters of these two dramatists are slight work in comparison with Shakespeare's best—Falstaff has a third dimension and Epicure Mammon has only two. But this slightness is part of the nature of the art which Jonson practised, a smaller art than Shakespeare's. The inferiority of Massinger to Jonson is an inferiority, not of one type of art to another, but within Jonson's type. It is a simple deficiency. Marlowe's and Jonson's comedies were a view of life; they were, as great literature is, the transformation of a personality into a personal work of art, their lifetime's work, long or short. Massinger is not simply a smaller personality: his personality hardly exists. He did not, out of his own personality, build a world of art, as Shakespeare and Marlowe and Jonson built.

In the fine pages which Remy de Gourmont devotes to Flaubert in his *Problème du Style,* the great critic declares:

La vie est un dépouillement. Le but de l'activité propre de l'homme est de nettoyer sa personnalité, de la laver de toutes les souillures qu'y déposa l'éducation, de la dégager de toutes les empreintes qu'y laissèrent nos admirations adolescentes;

and again:

Flaubert incorporait toute sa sensibilité à ses œuvres.... Hors de ses livres, où il se transvasait goutte à goutte, jusqu'à la lie, Flaubert est fort peu intéressant....

Of Shakespeare notably, of Jonson less, of Marlowe (and of Keats to the term of life allowed him), one can say that they *se transvasaient goutte à goutte;* and in England, which has produced a prodigious number of men of genius and comparatively few works of art, there are not many writers of whom one can say it. Certainly not of Massinger. A brilliant master of technique, he was not, in this profound sense, an artist. And so we come to inquire how, if this is so, he could have written two great comedies. We shall probably be obliged to conclude that a large part of their excellence is, in some way which should be defined, fortuitous; and that therefore they are, however remarkable, not works of perfect art.

This objection raised by Leslie Stephen to Massinger's method of revealing a villain has great cogency; but I am inclined to believe that the cogency is due to a somewhat different reason from that which Leslie Stephen assigns. His statement is too *apriorist* to be quite trustworthy. There is no reason why a comedy or tragedy villain should not declare himself, and in as long a period as the author likes; but the sort of villain who may run on in this way is a simple villain (simple not *simpliste*). Barabas and Volpone can declare their character, because they have no inside; appearance and reality are coincident; they are forces in particular directions. Massinger's two villains are not simple. Giles Overreach is essentially a great force directed upon small objects; a great force, a small mind; the terror of a dozen parishes instead of

the conqueror of a world. The force is misapplied, attenu-
ated, thwarted, by the man's vulgarity: he is a great man of
the City, without fear, but with the most abject awe of the
aristocracy. He is accordingly not simple, but a product of a
certain civilization, and he is not wholly conscious. His mono-
logues are meant to be, not what he thinks he is, but what he
really is: and yet they are not the truth about him, and he him-
self certainly does not know the truth. To declare himself,
therefore, is impossible.

> Nay, when my ears are pierced with widows' cries,
> And undone orphans wash with tears my threshold,
> I only think what 'tis to have my daughter
> Right honourable; and 'tis a powerful charm
> Makes me insensible of remorse, or pity,
> Or the least sting of conscience.

This is the wrong note. Elsewhere we have the right:

> Thou art a fool;
> In being out of office, I am out of danger;
> Where, if I were a justice, besides the trouble,
> I might or out of wilfulness, or error,
> Run myself finely into a praemunire,
> And so become a prey to the informer,
> No, I'll have none of 't; 'tis enough I keep
> Greedy at my devotion: so he serve
> My purposes, let him hang, or damn, I care not . . .

And how well tuned, well modulated, here, the diction! The
man is audible and visible. But from passages like the first we
may be permitted to infer that Massinger was unconscious of
trying to develop a different kind of character from any that
Marlowe or Jonson had invented.

Luke Frugal, in *The City Madam*, is not so great a character
as Sir Giles Overreach. But Luke Frugal just misses being al-
most the greatest of all hypocrites. His humility in the first act

of the play is more than half real. The error in his portraiture is not the extravagant hocus-pocus of supposed Indian necromancers by which he is so easily duped, but the premature disclosure of villainy in his temptation of the two apprentices of his brother. But for this, he would be a perfect chameleon of circumstance. Here, again, we feel that Massinger was conscious only of inventing a rascal of the old simpler farce type. But the play is not a farce, in the sense in which *The Jew of Malta, The Alchemist, Bartholomew Fair* are farces. Massinger had not the personality to create great farce, and he was too serious to invent trivial farce. The ability to perform that slight distortion of *all* the elements in the world of a play or a story, so that this world is complete in itself, which was given to Marlowe and Jonson (and to Rabelais) and which is prerequisite to great farce, was denied to Massinger. On the other hand, his temperament was more closely related to theirs than to that of Shirley or the Restoration wits. His two comedies therefore occupy a place by themselves. His ways of thinking and feeling isolate him from both the Elizabethan and the later Caroline mind. He might almost have been a great realist; he is killed by conventions which were suitable for the preceding literary generation, but not for his. Had Massinger been a greater man, a man of more intellectual courage, the current of English literature immediately after him might have taken a different course. The defect is precisely a defect of personality. He is not, however, the only man of letters who, at the moment when a new view of life is wanted, has looked at life through the eyes of his predecessors, and only at manners through his own.

SWINBURNE AS POET

It is a question of some nicety to decide how much must be read of any particular poet. And it is not a question merely of the size of the poet. There are some poets whose every line has unique value. There are others who can be taken by a few poems universally agreed upon. There are others who need be read only in selections, but what selections are read will not very much matter. Of Swinburne, we should like to have the *Atalanta* entire, and a volume of selections which should certainly contain *The Leper, Laus Veneris,* and *The Triumph of Time.* It ought to contain many more, but there is perhaps no other single poem which it would be an error to omit. A student of Swinburne will want to read one of the Stuart plays and dip into *Tristram of Lyonesse.* But almost no one, to-day, will wish to read the whole of Swinburne. It is not because Swinburne is voluminous; certain poets, equally voluminous, must be read entire. The necessity and the difficulty of a selection are due to the peculiar nature of Swinburne's contribution, which, it is hardly too much to say, is of a very different kind from that of any other poet of equal reputation.

We may take it as undisputed that Swinburne did make a contribution; that he did something that had not been done before, and that what he did will not turn out to be a fraud. And from that we may proceed to inquire what Swinburne's contribution was, and why, whatever critical solvents we employ to break down the structure of his verse, this contribution remains. The test is this: agreed that we do not (and I think that the present generation does not) greatly enjoy Swinburne, and agreed that (a more serious condemnation) at one period of our lives we did enjoy him and now no longer enjoy him; nevertheless, the words which we use to state our grounds of dislike or indifference cannot be applied to Swinburne as they can to bad poetry. The words of condemnation are words which express his qualities. You may say "diffuse." But the diffuseness is essential; had Swinburne practised greater concentration his verse would be, not better in the same kind, but a different thing. His diffuseness is one of his glories. That so little material as appears to be employed in *The Triumph of Time* should release such an amazing number of words, requires what there is no reason to call anything but genius. You could not condense *The Triumph of Time*. You could only leave out. And this would destroy the poem; though no one stanza seems essential. Similarly, a considerable quantity—a volume of selections—is necessary to give the quality of Swinburne although there is perhaps no one poem essential in this selection.

If, then, we must be very careful in applying terms of censure, like "diffuse," we must be equally careful of praise. "The beauty of Swinburne's verse is the sound," people say, explaining, "he had little visual imagination." I am inclined to think that the word "beauty" is hardly to be used in connection with Swinburne's verse at all; but in any case the beauty or effect of sound is neither that of music nor that of poetry which can be set to music. There is no reason why verse intended to be sung should not present a sharp visual image or convey an important intellectual meaning, for it supplements the music by another means of affecting the feelings. What we get in Swinburne is an expression by sound, which could not possibly associate itself with music. For what he gives is not images and ideas and music, it is one thing with a curious mixture of suggestions of all three.

> Shall I come, if I swim? wide are the waves, you see;
> Shall I come, if I fly, my dear Love, to thee?

This is Campion, and an example of the kind of music that is not to be found in Swinburne. It is an arrangement and choice of words which has a sound-value and at the same time a coherent comprehensible meaning, and the two things—the musical value and meaning—are two things, not one. But in Swinburne, there is no *pure* beauty—no pure beauty of sound, or of image, or of idea.

> Music, when soft voices die,
> Vibrates in the memory;
> Odours, when sweet violets sicken,
> Live within the sense they quicken.
>
> Rose leaves, when the rose is dead,
> Are heaped for the beloved's bed;
> And so thy thoughts, when thou art gone,
> Love itself shall slumber on.

I quote from Shelley, because Shelley is supposed to be the master of Swinburne; and because his song, like that of Campion, has what Swinburne has not—a beauty of music and a beauty of content; and because it is clearly and simply expressed, with only two adjectives. Now, in Swinburne the meaning and the sound are one thing. He is concerned with the meaning of the word in a peculiar way: he employs, or rather "works," the word's meaning. And this is connected with an interesting fact about his vocabulary: he uses the most general word, because his emotion is never particular, never in direct line of vision, never focused; it is emotion reinforced, not by intensification, but by expansion.

> There lived a singer in France of old
> By the tideless dolorous midland sea.

> In a land of sand and ruin and gold
> There shone one woman, and none but she.

You see that Provence is the merest point of diffusion here. Swinburne defines the place by the most general word, which has for him its own value. "Gold," "ruin," "dolorous": it is not merely the sound that he wants, but the vague associations of idea that the words give him. He has not his eye on a particular place, as

> Li ruscelletti che dei verdi colli
> Del Casentin discendon giuso in Arno ...

It is, in fact, the word that gives him the thrill, not the object. When you take to pieces any verse of Swinburne, you find always that the object was not there—only the word. Compare

> Snowdrops that plead for pardon
> And pine for fright

with the daffodils that come before the swallow dares. The snowdrop of Swinburne disappears, the daffodil of Shakespeare remains. The swallow of Shakespeare remain in the verse in *Macbeth*; the bird of Wordsworth

> Breaking the silence of the seas

remains; the swallow of "Itylus" disappears. Compare, again, a chorus of *Atalanta* with a chorus from Athenian tragedy. The chorus of Swinburne is almost a parody of the Athenian: it is sententious, but it has not even the significance of commonplace.

> At least we witness of thee ere we die
> That these things are not otherwise, but thus. ...

Before the beginning of years
    There came to the making of man
Time with a gift of tears;
    Grief with a glass that ran. . . .

This is not merely "music"; it is effective because it appears to be a tremendous statement, like statements made in our dreams; when we wake up we find that the "glass that ran" would do better for time than for grief, and that the gift of tears would be as appropriately bestowed by grief as by time.

It might seem to be intimated, by what has been said, that the work of Swinburne can be shown to be a sham, just as bad verse is a sham. It would only be so if you could produce or suggest something that it pretends to be and is not. The world of Swinburne does not depend upon some other world which it simulates; it has the necessary completeness and self-sufficiency for justification and permanence. It is impersonal, and no one else could have made it. The deductions are true to the postulates. It is indestructible. None of the obvious complaints that were or might have been brought to bear upon the first *Poems and Ballads* holds good. The poetry is not morbid, it is not erotic, it is not destructive. These are adjectives which can be applied to the material, the human feelings, which in Swinburne's case do not exist. The morbidity is not of human feeling but of language. Language in a healthy state presents the object, is so close to the object that the two are identified.

They are identified in the verse of Swinburne solely because the object has ceased to exist, because the meaning is merely the hallucination of meaning, because language, uprooted, has adapted itself to an independent life of atmospheric nourishment. In Swinburne, for example, we see the word "weary" flourishing in this way independent of the particular and actual weariness of flesh or spirit. The bad poet dwells partly in a world of objects and partly in a world of words, and he never can get them to fit. Only a man of genius could dwell so exclusively and consistently among words as Swinburne. His language is not, like the language of bad poetry, dead. It is very much alive, with this singular life of its own. But the language which is more important to us is that which is struggling to digest and express new objects, new groups of objects, new feelings, new aspects, as, for instance, the prose of Mr. James Joyce or the earlier Conrad.

BLAKE

I

If one follow Blake's mind through the several stages of his poetic development it is impossible to regard him as a naïf, a wild man, a wild pet for the supercultivated. The strangeness is evaporated, the peculiarity is seen to be the peculiarity of all great poetry: something which is found (not everywhere) in Homer and Æschylus and Dante and Villon, and profound and concealed in the work of Shakespeare—and also in another form in Montaigne and in Spinoza. It is merely a peculiar honesty, which, in a world too frightened to be honest, is peculiarly terrifying. It is an honesty against which the whole world conspires, because it is unpleasant. Blake's poetry has the unpleasantness of great poetry. Nothing that can be called morbid or abnormal or perverse, none of the things which exemplify the sickness of an epoch or a fashion, have this quality; only those things which, by some extraordinary labour of simplification, exhibit the essential sickness or strength of the human soul. And this honesty never exists without great technical accomplishment. The question about Blake the man is the question of the circumstances that concurred to permit this honesty in his work, and what circumstances define its limitations. The favouring conditions probably include these two: that, being early apprenticed to a manual occupation, he

was not compelled to acquire any other education in litera-
ture than he wanted, or to acquire it for any other reason than
that he wanted it; and that, being a humble engraver, he had
no journalistic-social career open to him.

There was, that is to say, nothing to distract him from his
interests or to corrupt these interests: neither the ambitions of
parents or wife, nor the standards of society, nor the tempta-
tions of success; nor was he exposed to imitation of himself or
of anyone else. These circumstances—not his supposed in-
spired and untaught spontaneity—are what make him inno-
cent. His early poems show what the poems of a boy of genius
ought to show, immense power of assimilation. Such early
poems are not, as usually supposed, crude attempts to do
something beyond the boy's capacity; they are, in the case of
a boy of real promise, more likely to be quite mature and suc-
cessful attempts to do something small. So with Blake, his
early poems are technically admirable, and their originality is
in an occasional rhythm. The verse of *Edward III* deserves
study. But his affection for certain Elizabethans is not so sur-
prising as his affinity with the very best work of his own cen-
tury. He is very like Collins, he is very eighteenth century.
The poem *Whether on Ida's shady brow* is eighteenth-century
work; the movement, the weight of it, the syntax, the choice
of words—

> The *languid* strings do scarcely move!
> The sound is *forc'd*, the notes are few!

this is contemporary with Gray and Collins, it is the poetry of
a language which has undergone the discipline of prose.
Blake up to twenty is decidedly a traditional.

Blake's beginnings as a poet, then, are as normal as the be-
ginnings of Shakespeare. His method of composition, in his
mature work, is exactly like that of other poets. He has an
idea (a feeling, an image), he develops it by accretion or ex-
pansion, alters his verse often, and hesitates often over the

final choice.[1] The idea, of course, simply comes, but upon arrival it is subjected to prolonged manipulation. In the first phase Blake is concerned with verbal beauty; in the second he becomes the apparent naïf, really the mature intelligence. It is only when the ideas become more automatic, come more freely and are less manipulated, that we begin to suspect their origin, to suspect that they spring from a shallower source.

The Songs of Innocence and of Experience, and the poems from the Rossetti manuscript, are the poems of a man with a profound interest in human emotions, and a profound knowledge of them. The emotions are presented in an extremely simplified, abstract form. This form is one illustration of the external struggle of art against education, of the literary artist against the continuous deterioration of language.

It is important that the artist should be highly educated in his own art; but his education is one that is hindered rather than helped by the ordinary processes of society which constitute education for the ordinary man. For these processes consist largely in the acquisition of impersonal ideas which obscure what we really are and feel, what we really want, and what really excites our interest. It is of course not the actual information acquired, but the conformity which the accumulation of knowledge is apt to impose, that is harmful. Tennyson is a very fair example of a poet almost wholly encrusted with parasitic opinion, almost wholly merged into his environment. Blake, on the other hand, knew what interested him, and he therefore presents only the essential, only, in fact, what can be presented, and need not be explained. And because he was not distracted, or frightened, or occupied in anything but

---

[1] I do not know why M. Berger should say, without qualification, in his *William Blake: mysticisme et poésie,* that "son respect pour l'esprit qui soufflait en lui et qui dictait ses paroles l'empêchait de les corriger jamais." Dr. Sampson, in his Oxford edition of Blake, gives us to understand that Blake believed much of his writing to be automatic, but observes that Blake's "meticulous care in composition is everywhere apparent in the poems preserved in rough draft . . . alteration on alteration, rearrangement after rearrangement, deletions, additions, and inversions. . . ."

exact statement, he understood. He was naked, and saw man naked, and from the centre of his own crystal. To him there was no more reason why Swedenborg should be absurd than Locke. He accepted Swedenborg, and eventually rejected him, for reasons of his own. He approached everything with a mind unclouded by current opinions. There was nothing of the superior person about him. This makes him terrifying.

II

But if there was nothing to distract him from sincerity there were, on the other hand, the dangers to which the naked man is exposed. His philosophy, like his visions, like his insight, like his technique, was his own. And accordingly he was inclined to attach more importance to it than an artist should; this is what makes him eccentric, and makes him inclined to formlessness.

> But most through midnight streets I hear
> How the youthful harlot's curse
> Blasts the new-born infant's tear,
> And blights with plagues the marriage hearse,

is the naked vision;

> Love seeketh only self to please,
> To bind another to its delight,
> Joys in another's loss of ease,
> And builds a Hell in Heaven's despite,

is the naked observation; and *The Marriage of Heaven and Hell* is naked philosophy, presented. But Blake's occasional marriages of poetry and philosophy are not so felicitous.

> He who would do good to another must do it in Minute
> Particulars

> General Good is the plea of the scoundrel, hypocrite, and
> flatterer;
> For Art and Science cannot exist but in minutely organized
> particulars. . . .

One feels that the form is not well chosen. The borrowed phi-
losophy of Dante and Lucretius is perhaps not so interesting,
but it injures their form less. Blake did not have that more
Mediterranean gift of form which knows how to borrow as
Dante borrowed his theory of the soul; he must needs create
a philosophy as well as a poetry. A similar formlessness at-
tacks his draughtsmanship. The fault is most evident, of
course, in the longer poems—or rather, the poems in which
structure is important. You cannot create a very large poem
without introducing a more impersonal point of view, or
splitting it up into various personalities. But the weakness of
the long poems is certainly not that they are too visionary, too
remote from the world. It is that Blake did not see enough, be-
came too much occupied with ideas.

We have the same respect for Blake's philosophy (and per-
haps for that of Samuel Butler) that we have for an ingenious
piece of home-made furniture: we admire the man who has
put it together out of the odds and ends about the house.
England has produced a fair number of these resourceful
Robinson Crusoes; but we are not really so remote from the
Continent, or from our own past, as to be deprived of the
advantages of culture if we wish them.

We may speculate, for amusement, whether it would not
have been beneficial to the north of Europe generally, and to
Britain in particular, to have had a more continuous religious
history. The local divinities of Italy were not wholly extermi-
nated by Christianity, and they were not reduced to the
dwarfish fate which fell upon our trolls and pixies. The latter,
with the major Saxon deities, were perhaps no great loss in
themselves, but they left an empty place; and perhaps our
mythology was further impoverished by the divorce from

Rome. Milton's celestial and infernal regions are large but insufficiently furnished apartments filled by heavy conversation; and one remarks about the Puritan mythology an historical thinness. And about Blake's supernatural territories, as about the supposed ideas that dwell there, we cannot help commenting on a certain meanness of culture. They illustrate the crankiness, the eccentricity, which frequently affects writers outside of the Latin traditions, and which such a critic as Arnold should certainly have rebuked. And they are not essential to Blake's inspiration.

Blake was endowed with a capacity for considerable understanding of human nature, with a remarkable and original sense of language and the music of language, and a gift of hallucinated vision. Had these been controlled by a respect for impersonal reason, for common sense, for the objectivity of science, it would have been better for him. What his genius required, and what it sadly lacked, was a framework of accepted and traditional ideas which would have prevented him from indulging in a philosophy of his own, and concentrated his attention upon the problems of the poet. Confusion of thought, emotion, and vision is what we find in such a work as *Also Sprach Zarathustra;* it is eminently not a Latin virtue. The concentration resulting from a framework of mythology and theology and philosophy is one of the reasons why Dante is a classic, and Blake only a poet of genius. The fault is perhaps not with Blake himself, but with the environment which failed to provide what such a poet needed; perhaps the circumstances compelled him to fabricate, perhaps the poet required the philosopher and mythologist; although the conscious Blake may have been quite unconscious of the motives.

DANTE

M. Paul Valéry, a writer for whom I have considerable respect, has placed in his most recent statement upon poetry a paragraph which seems to me of very doubtful validity. I have not seen the complete essay, and know the quotation only as it appears in a critical notice in the *Athenæum*, July 23, 1920:

> La philosophie, et même la morale tendirent à fuir les œuvres pour se placer dans les réflexions qui les précèdent.... Parler aujourd'hui de poésie philosophique (fût-ce en invoquant Alfred de Vigny, Leconte de Lisle, et quelques autres), c'est naivement confondre des conditions et des applications de l'esprit incompatibles entre elles. N'est-ce pas oublier que le but de celui qui spécule est de fixer ou de créer une notion—c'est-à-dire un *pouvoir* et un *instrument de pouvoir*, cependant que le poète moderne essaie de produire en nous un *état* et de porter cet état exceptionnel au point d'une jouissance parfaite....

It may be that I do M. Valéry an injustice which I must endeavour to repair when I have the pleasure of reading his article entire. But the paragraph gives the impression of more than one error of analysis. In the first place, it suggests that conditions have changed, that "philosophical" poetry may once have been permissible, but that (perhaps owing to the

greater specialization of the modern world) it is now intoler-
able. We are forced to assume that what we do not like in our
time was never good art, and that what appears to us good was
always so. If any ancient "philosophical" poetry retains its
value, a value which we fail to find in modern poetry of the
same type, we investigate on the assumption that we shall find
some difference to which the mere difference of date is irrel-
evant. But if it be maintained that the older poetry has a
"philosophic" element and a "poetic" element which can be
isolated, we have two tasks to perform. We must show first in
a particular case—our case is Dante—that the philosophy is
essential to the structure and that the structure is essential to
the poetic beauty of the parts; and we must show that the phi-
losophy is employed in a different form from that which it
takes in admittedly unsuccessful philosophical poems. And if
M. Valéry is in error in his complete exorcism of "philoso-
phy," perhaps the basis of the error is his apparently com-
mendatory interpretation of the effort of the modern poet,
namely, that the latter endeavours "to produce in us a *state*."

The early philosophical poets, Parmenides and Empedo-
cles, were apparently persons of an impure philosophical in-
spiration. Neither their predecessors nor their successors
expressed themselves in verse; Parmenides and Empedocles
were persons who mingled with genuine philosophical ability
a good deal of the emotion of the founder of a second-rate
religious system. They were not interested exclusively in phi-
losophy, or religion, or poetry, but in something which was a
mixture of all three; hence their reputation as poets is low
and as philosophers should be considerably below Heraclitus,
Zeno, Anaxagoras, or Democritus. The poem of Lucretius is
quite a different matter. For Lucretius was undoubtedly a
poet. He endeavours to expound a philosophical system, but
with a different motive from Parmenides or Empedocles, for
this system is already in existence; he is really endeavouring
to find the concrete poetic equivalent for this system—to find

its complete equivalent in vision. Only, as he is an innovator in this art, he wavers between philosophical poetry and philosophy. So we find passages such as:

> But the velocity of thunderbolts is great and their stroke powerful, and they run through their course with a rapid descent, because the force when aroused first in all cases collects itself in the clouds and . . . Let us now sing what causes the motion of the stars. . . . Of all these different smells then which strike the nostrils one may reach to a much greater distance than another. . . .[1]

But Lucretius' true tendency is to express an ordered vision of the life of man, with great vigour of real poetic image and often acute observation.

> quod petiere, premunt arte faciuntque dolorem
> corporis et dentes inlidunt saepe labellis
> osculaque adfligunt, quia non est pura voluptas
> et stimuli subsunt qui instigant laedere id ipsum
> quodcumque est, rabies unde illaec germina surgunt . . .

>   medio de fonte leporum
> surgit amari aliquid quod in ipsis floribus angat . . .

> nec procumbere humi prostratum et pandere palmas
> ante deum delubra nec aras sanguine multo
> spargere quadrupedum nec votis nectere vota,
> sed mage pacata posse omnia mente tueri.

The philosophy which Lucretius tackled was not rich enough in variety of feeling, applied itself to life too uniformly, to supply the material for a wholly successful poem. It was incapable of complete expansion into pure vision. But I must ask M. Valéry whether the "aim" of Lucretius' poem was "to fix or create a notion" or to fashion "an instrument of power."

[1] Munro's translation, *passim*.

Without doubt, the effort of the philosopher proper, the man who is trying to deal with ideas in themselves, and the effort of the poet, who may be trying to *realize* ideas, cannot be carried on at the same time. But this is not to deny that poetry can be in some sense philosophic. The poet can deal with philosophic ideas, not as matter for argument, but as matter for inspection. The original form of a philosophy cannot be poetic. But poetry can be penetrated by a philosophic idea, it can deal with this idea when it has reached the point of immediate acceptance, when it has become almost a physical modification. If we divorced poetry and philosophy altogether, we should bring a serious impeachment, not only against Dante, but against most of Dante's contemporaries.

Dante had the benefit of a mythology and a theology which had undergone a more complete absorption into life than those of Lucretius. It is curious that not only Dante's detractors, like the Petrarch of Landor's *Pentameron* (if we may apply so strong a word to so amiable a character), but some of his admirers, insist on the separation of Dante's "poetry" and Dante's "teaching." Sometimes the philosophy is confused with the allegory. The philosophy is an ingredient, it is a part of Dante's world just as it is a part of life; the allegory is the scaffold on which the poem is built. An American writer of a little primer of Dante, Mr. Henry Dwight Sidgwick, who desires to improve our understanding of Dante as a "spiritual leader," says:

> To Dante this literal Hell was a secondary matter; so it is to us. He and we are concerned with the allegory. That allegory is simple. Hell is the absence of God. . . . If the reader begins with the consciousness that he is reading about sin, spiritually understood, he never loses the thread, he is never at a loss, never slips back into the literal signification.

Without stopping to question Mr. Sidgwick on the difference between literal and spiritual sin, we may affirm that his remarks are misleading. Undoubtedly the allegory is to be taken seriously, and certainly the *Comedy* is in some way a "moral education." The question is to find a formula for the correspondence between the former and the latter, to decide whether the moral value corresponds directly to the allegory. We can easily ascertain what importance Dante assigned to allegorical method. In the *Convivio* we are serious informed that

> the principle design [of the odes] is to lead men to knowledge and virtue, as will be seen in the progress of the truth of them;

and we are also given the familiar four interpretations of an ode: literal, allegorical, moral, and anagogical. And so distinguished a scholar as M. Hauvette repeats again and again the phrase "didactique d'intention." We accept the allegory. Accepted, there are two usual ways of dealing with it. One may, with Mr. Sidgwick, dwell upon its significance for the seeker of "spiritual light," or one may, with Landor, deplore the spiritual mechanics and find the poet only in passages where he frees himself from his divine purposes. With neither of these points of view can we concur. Mr. Sidgwick magnifies the "preacher and prophet," and presents Dante as a superior Isaiah or Carlyle; Landor reserves the poet, reprehends the scheme, and denounces the politics. Some of Landor's errors are more palpable than Mr. Sidgwick's. He errs, in the first place, in judging Dante by the standards of classical epic. Whatever the *Comedy* is, an epic it is not. M. Hauvette well says:

> Rechercher dans quelle mesure le poème se rapproche du genre classique de l'épopée, et dans quelle mesure il s'en écarte, est un exércice de rhétorique entièrement inutile, puisque Dante, à n'en pas douter, n'a jamais eu l'intention de composer une action épique dans les règles.

But we must define the framework of Dante's poem from the result as well as from the intention. The poem has not only a framework, but a form; and even if the framework be allegorical, the form may be something else. The examination of any episode in the *Comedy* ought to show that not merely the allegorical interpretation or the didactic intention, but the emotional significance itself, cannot be isolated from the rest of the poem. Landor appears, for instance, to have misunderstood such a passage as the Paolo and Francesca, by failing to perceive its relations:

> In the midst of her punishment, Francesca, when she comes to the tenderest part of her story, tells it with complacency and delight.

This is surely a false simplification. To have lost all recollected delight would have been, for Francesca, either loss of humanity or relief from damnation. The ecstasy, with the present thrill at the remembrance of it, is a part of the torture. Francesca is neither stupefied nor reformed; she is merely damned; and it is a part of damnation to experience desires that we can no longer gratify. For in Dante's Hell souls are not deadened, as they mostly are in life; they are actually in the greatest torment of which each is capable.

E il modo ancor m'offende.

It is curious that Mr. Sidgwick, whose approbation is at the opposite pole from Landor's, should have fallen into a similar error. He says:

> In meeting [Ulysses], as in meeting Pier della Vigna and Brunetto Latini, the preacher and the prophet are lost in the poet.

Here, again, is a false simplification. These passages have no digressive beauty. The case of Brunetto is parallel to that of

Francesca. The emotion of the passage resides in Brunetto's excellence in damnation—so admirable a soul, and so perverse.

> e parve de costoro
> Quegli che vince e non colui che perde.

And I think that if Mr. Sidgwick had pondered the strange words of Ulysses,

> com' altrui piacque,

he would not have said that the preacher and prophet are lost in the poet. "Preacher" and "prophet" are odious terms; but what Mr. Sidgwick designates by them is something which is certainly not "lost in the poet," but is part of the poet.

A variety of passages might illustrate the assertion that no emotion is contemplated by Dante purely in and for itself. The emotion of the person, or the emotion with which our attitude appropriately invests the person, is never lost or diminished, is always preserved entire, but is modified by the position assigned to the person in the eternal scheme, is coloured by the atmosphere of that person's residence in one of the three worlds. About none of Dante's characters is there that ambiguity which affects Milton's Lucifer. The damned preserve any degree of beauty or grandeur that ever rightly pertained to them, and this intensifies and also justifies their damnation. As Jason

> Guarda quel grande che viene!
> E per dolor non par lagrima spanda,
> Quanto aspetto reale ancor ritiene!

The crime of Bertrand becomes more lurid; the vindictive Adamo acquires greater ferocity, and the errors of Arnaut are corrected—

Poi s'ascose nel foco che gli affina.

If the artistic emotion presented by any episode of the *Comedy* is dependent upon the whole, we may proceed to inquire what the whole scheme is. The usefulness of allegory and astronomy is obvious. A mechanical framework, in a poem of so vast an ambit, was a necessity. As the centre of gravity of emotions is more remote from a single human action, or a system of purely human actions, than in drama or epic, so the framework has to be more artificial and apparently more mechanical. It is not essential that the allegory or the almost unintelligible astronomy should be understood—only that its presence should be justified. The emotional structure within this scaffold is what must be understood—the structure made possible by the scaffold. This structure is an ordered scale of human emotions. Not, necessarily, *all* human emotions; and in any case all the emotions are limited, and also extended in significance by their place in the scheme.

But Dante's is the most comprehensive, and the most *ordered* presentation of emotions that has ever been made. Dante's method of dealing with any emotion may be contrasted, not so appositely with that of other "epic" poets as with that of Shakespeare. Shakespeare takes a character apparently controlled by a simple emotion, and analyses the character and the emotion itself. The emotion is split up into constituents—and perhaps destroyed in the process. The mind of Shakespeare was one of the most *critical* that has ever existed. Dante, on the other hand, does not analyse the emotion so much as he exhibits its relation to the other emotions. You cannot, that is, understand the *Inferno* without the *Purgatorio* and the *Paradiso*. "Dante," says Landor's Petrarch, "is the great master of the disgusting." That is true, though Sophocles at least once approaches him. But a disgust like Dante's is no hypertrophy of a single reaction: it is completed and explained only by the last canto of the Paradiso.

> La forma universal di questo nodo
> credo ch'io vidi, perchè più di largo
>   dicendo questo, mi sento ch'io godo.

The contemplation of the horrid or sordid or disgusting, by an artist, is the necessary and negative aspect of the impulse toward the pursuit of beauty. But not all succeed as did Dante in expressing the complete scale from negative to positive. The negative is the more importunate.

The structure of emotions, for which the allegory is the necessary scaffold, is complete from the most sensuous to the most intellectual and the most spiritual. Dante gives a concrete presentation of the most elusive:

> Pareva a me che nube ne coprisse
> lucida, spessa, solida e polita,
>   quasi adamante che lo sol ferisse.

> Per entro sè l'eterna margarita
> ne recepette, com' acqua recepe
>   raggio di luce, permanendo unita.

or

> Nel suo aspetto tal dentro mi fei,
> qual si fe' Glauco nel gustar dell' erba,
>   che il fe' consorto in mar degli altri dei.[1]

Again, in the *Purgatorio,* for instance in Canto XVI and Canto XVIII, occur passages of pure exposition of philosophy, the philosophy of Aristotle strained through the schools.

> Lo natural e sempre senza errore,
> ma l' altro puote errar per malo obbietto,
>   o per poco o per troppo di vigore . . .

[1] See E. Pound, *The Spirit of Romance,* p. 145.

We are not here studying the philosophy, we *see* it, as part of the ordered world. The aim of the poet is to state a vision, and no vision of life can be complete which does not include the articulate formulation of life which human minds make.

Onde convenne legge per fren porre . . .

It is one of the greatest merits of Dante's poem that the vision is so nearly complete; it is evidence of this greatness that the significance of any single passage, of any of the passages that are selected as "poetry," is incomplete unless we ourselves apprehend the whole.

And Dante helps us to provide a criticism of M. Valéry's "modern poet" who attempts "to produce in us a *state*." A state, in itself, is nothing whatever.

M. Valéry's account is quite in harmony with pragmatic doctrine, and with the tendencies of such a work as William James's *Varieties of Religious Experience*. The mystical experience is supposed to be valuable because it is a pleasant state of unique intensity. But the true mystic is not satisfied merely by feeling, he must pretend at least that he *sees*, and the absorption into the divine is only the necessary, if paradoxical, limit of this contemplation. The poet does not aim to excite—that is not even a test of his success—but to set something down; the state of the reader is merely that reader's particular mode of perceiving what the poet has caught in words. Dante, more than any other poet, has succeeded in dealing with his philosophy, not as a theory (in the modern and not the Greek sense of that word) or as his own comment or reflection, but in terms of something *perceived*. When most of our modern poets confine themselves to what they had perceived, they produce for us, usually, only odds and ends of still life and stage properties; but that does not imply so much that the method of Dante is obsolete, as that our vision is perhaps comparatively restricted.

NOTE.—My friend the Abbé Laban has reproached me for attributing to Landor, in this essay, sentiments which are merely the expression of his dramatic figure Petrarch, and which imply rather Landor's reproof of the limitations of the historical Petrarch's view of Dante, than the view of Landor himself. The reader should therefore observe this correction of my use of Landor's honoured name.

ANDREW MARVELL

The tercentenary of the former member for Hull deserves not only the celebration proposed by that favoured borough, but a little serious reflection upon his writing. That is an act of piety, which is very different from the resurrection of a deceased reputation. Marvell has stood high for some years; his best poems are not very many, and not only must be well known, from the "Golden Treasury" and the "Oxford Book of English Verse," but must also have been enjoyed by numerous readers. His grave needs neither rose nor rue nor laurel; there is no imaginary justice to be done; we may think about him, if there be need for thinking, for our own benefit, not his. To bring the poet back to life—the great, the perennial, task of criticism—is in this case to squeeze the drops of the essence of two or three poems; even confining ourselves to these, we may find some precious liquor unknown to the present age. Not to determine rank, but to isolate this quality, is the critical labour. The fact that of all Marvell's verse, which is itself not a great quantity, the really valuable part consists of a very few poems indicates that the unknown quality of which we speak is probably a literary rather than a personal quality; or, more truly, that it is a quality of a civilization, of a traditional habit of life. A poet like Donne, or like Baudelaire or Laforgue, may almost be considered the inventor of an attitude, a system of feeling or of morals. Donne is difficult to analyse: what appears at one time a curious personal point of view may at another time appear rather the precise concentration of a kind of feeling diffused in the air about him. Donne and his shroud, the shroud and his motive for wearing it, are inseparable, but they are not the same thing. The seventeenth century sometimes seems for more than a moment to gather up and to digest into its art all the experience of the human mind which (from the same point of view) the later centuries seem to have been partly engaged in repudiating. But Donne would have been an individual at any time and place; Marvell's best verse is the product of European, that is to say Latin, culture.

Out of that high style developed from Marlowe through Jonson (for Shakespeare does not lend himself to these genealogies) the seventeenth century separated two qualities: wit and magniloquence. Neither is as simple or as apprehensible as its name seems to imply, and the two are not in practice antithetical; both are conscious and cultivated, and the mind which cultivates one may cultivate the other. The actual poetry, of Marvell, of Cowley, of Milton and of others, is a blend in varying proportions. And we must be on guard not to employ the terms with too wide a comprehension; for like the other fluid terms with which literary criticism deals, the meaning alters with the age, and for precision we must rely to some degree upon the literacy and good taste of the reader. The wit of the Caroline poets is not the wit of Shakespeare, and it is not the wit of Dryden, the great master of contempt, or of Pope, the great master of hatred, or of Swift, the great master of disgust. What is meant is something which is a common quality to the songs in *Comus* and Cowley's Anacreontics and Marvell's Horatian Ode. It is more than a technical accomplishment, or the vocabulary and syntax of an epoch; it is, what we have designated tentatively as wit, a tough reasonableness beneath the slight lyric grace. You cannot find it in Shelley or Keats or Wordsworth; you cannot find more than an echo of it in Landor; still less in Tennyson or Browning;

and among contemporaries Mr. Yeats is an Irishman and Mr. Hardy is a modern Englishman—that is to say, Mr. Hardy is without it and Mr. Yeats is outside of the tradition altogether. On the other hand, as it certainly exists in Lafontaine, there is a large part of it in Gautier. And of the magniloquence, the deliberate exploitation of the possibilities of magnificence in language which Milton used and abused, there is also use and even abuse in the poetry of Baudelaire.

Wit is not a quality that we are accustomed to associate with "Puritan" literature, with Milton or with Marvell. But if so, we are at fault partly in our conception of wit and partly in our generalizations about the Puritans. And if the wit of Dryden or of Pope is not the only kind of wit in the language, the rest is not merely a little merriment or a little levity or a little impropriety or a little epigram. And, on the other hand, the sense in which a man like Marvell is a "Puritan" is restricted. The persons who opposed Charles I. and the persons who supported the Commonwealth were not all of the flock of Rabbi Zeal-of-the-land Busy or the United Grand Junction Ebenezer Temperance Association. Many of them were gentlemen of the time who merely believed, with considerable show of reason, that government by a Parliament of gentlemen was better than government by a Stuart; though they were, to that extent, Liberal Practitioners, they could hardly foresee the tea-meeting and the Dissidence of Dissent. Being men of education and culture, even of travel, some of them were exposed to that spirit of the age which was coming to be the French spirit of the age. This spirit, curiously enough, was quite opposed to the tendencies latent or the forces active in Puritanism; the contest does great damage to the poetry of Milton; Marvell, an active servant of the public, but a lukewarm partisan, and a poet on a smaller scale, is far less injured by it. His line on the statue of Charles II., "It is such a King as no chisel can mend," may be set off against his criticism of the Great Rebellion: "Men . . . ought and might have trusted the King." Marvell, therefore, more a man of the century than a Puritan, speaks more clearly and unequivocally with the voice of his literary age than does Milton.

This voice speaks out uncommonly strong in the "Coy Mistress." The theme is one of the great traditional commonplaces of European literature. It is the theme of "O mistress mine," of "Gather ye rosebuds," of "Go, lovely rose"; it is in the savage austerity of Lucretius and the intense levity of Catullus. Where the wit of Marvell renews the theme is in the variety and order of the images. In the first of the three paragraphs Marvell plays with a fancy which begins by pleasing and leads to astonishment.

> Had we but world enough and time,
> This coyness, lady, were no crime,
>   ... I would
> Love you ten years before the Flood,
> And you should, if you please, refuse
> Till the conversion of the Jews;
> My vegetable love should grow
> Vaster than empires and more slow. ...

We notice the high speed, the succession of concentrated images, each magnifying the original fancy. When this process has been carried to the end and summed up, the poem turns suddenly with that surprise which has been one of the most important means of poetic effect since Homer:—

> But at my back I always hear
> Time's wingèd chariot hurrying near,
> And yonder all before us lie
> Deserts of vast eternity.

A whole civilization resides in these lines:—

> Pallida Mors aequa pulsat pede pauperum tabernas,
> Regumque turris. . . .
> Eheu fugaces, Postume, Postume,
> Labuntur anni. . . .
> Post equitem sedet atra, Cura.

And not only Horace but Catullus himself:—

> Nobis, cum semel occidit brevis lux,
> Nox est perpetua una dormienda.

The verse of Marvell has not the grand reverberation of Catullus's Latin; but the image of Marvell is certainly more comprehensive and penetrates greater depths than any of those quoted from Horace.

A modern poet, had he reached the height, would very likely have closed on this moral reflection. But the three strophes of Marvell's poem have something like a syllogistic relation to each other. After a close approach to the mood of Donne,

> then worms shall try
> That long-preserved virginity . . .
> The grave's a fine and private place,
> But none, I think, do there embrace,

the conclusion,

> Let us roll all our strength and all
> Our sweetness up into one ball,
> And tear our pleasures with rough strife,
> Thorough the iron gates of life.

It will hardly be denied that this poem contains wit; but it may not be evident that this wit forms the crescendo and diminuendo of a scale of great imaginative power. The wit is not only combined with, but fused into, the imagination. We can easily recognize a witty fancy in the successive images ("my *vegetable* love," "till the conversion of the Jews"), but this fancy is not indulged, as it sometimes is by Cowley or Cleveland, for its own sake. It is structural decoration of a serious idea. In this it is superior to the fancy of "L'Allegro," "Il Penseroso," or the lighter and less successful poems of Keats. In fact, this alliance of levity and seriousness (by which the seriousness is intensified) is a characteristic of the sort of wit we are trying to identify. It is found in

> Le squelette était invisible
> Au temps heureux de l'art païen!

of Gautier, and in the *dandyisme* of Baudelaire and Laforgue. It is in the poem of Catullus which has been quoted, and in the variation by Ben Jonson:—

> Cannot we deceive the eyes
> Of a few poor household spies?
> 'Tis no sin love's fruits to steal,
> But that sweet sin to reveal,
> To be taken, to be seen,
> These have sins accounted been.

It is in Propertius and Ovid. It is a quality of a sophisticated literature; a quality which expands in English literature just at the moment before the English mind altered; it is not a quality which we should expect Puritanism to encourage. When we come to Gray and Collins, the sophistication remains only in the language, and has disappeared from the feeling. Gray and Collins were masters, but they had lost that hold on human values, that firm grasp of human experience, which is a formidable achievement of the Elizabethan and Jacobean poets. This wisdom, cynical perhaps but untired (in Shakespeare, a terrifying clairvoyance) leads toward, and is only completed by, the religious comprehension; it leads to the point of the *Ainsi tout leur a craqué dans la main* of Bouvard and Pécuchet.

The difference between imagination and fancy, in view of this poetry of wit, is a very narrow one. Obviously, an image which is immediately and unintentionally ridiculous is merely a fancy. In the poem "Upon Appleton House," Marvell falls in with one of these undesirable images, describing the attitude of the house toward its master:—

> Yet thus the laden house does sweat,
> And scarce endures the master great;
> But, where he comes, the swelling hall
> Stirs, and the square grows spherical;

which, whatever its intention, is more absurd than it was intended to be. Marvell also falls into the even commoner error of images which are overdeveloped or distracting; which support nothing but their own misshapen bodies:—

> And now the salmon-fishers moist
> Their leathern boats begin to hoist;
> And, like Antipodes in shoes,
> Have shod their heads in their canoes.

Of this sort of image a choice collection may be found in Johnson's "Life of Cowley." But the images in the "Coy Mistress" are not only witty, but satisfy the elucidation of Imagination given by Coleridge:—

> This power ... reveals itself in the balance or reconcilement of opposite or discordant qualities: of sameness, with difference; of the general, with the concrete; the idea with the image; the individual with the representative; the sense of novelty and freshness with old and familiar objects; a more than usual state of emotion with more than usual order; judgment ever awake and steady self-possession with enthusiasm and feeling profound or vehement....

Coleridge's statement applies also to the following verses, which are selected because of their similarity, and because they illustrate the marked caesura which Marvell often introduces in a short line:—

> The tawny mowers enter next,
> Who seem like Israelites to be
> Walking on foot through a green sea.

> And now the meadows fresher dyed,
> Whose grass, with moister colour dashed,
> Seems as green silks but newly washed.

> He hangs in shades the orange bright,
> Like golden lamps in a green night.

> Annihilating all that's made
> To a green thought in a green shade.

> Had it lived long, it would have been
> Lilies without, roses within.

The whole poem, from which the last of these quotations is drawn ("The Nymph and the Fawn"), is built upon a very slight foundation, and we can imagine what some of our modern practitioners of slight themes would have made of it. But we need not descend to an invidious contemporaneity to point the difference. Here are six lines from "The Nymph and the Fawn":—

> I have a garden of my own,
> But so with roses overgrown
> And lilies, that you would it guess
> To be a little wilderness;
> And all the spring-time of the year
> It only lovèd to be there.

And here are five lines from "The Nymph's Song to Hylas" in the "Life and Death of Jason," by William Morris:—

> I know a little garden close
> Set thick with lily and red rose.
> Where I would wander if I might
> From dewy dawn to dewy night,
> And have one with me wandering.

So far the resemblance is more striking than the difference, although we might just notice the vagueness of allusion in the last line to some indefinite person, form, or phantom, compared with the more explicit reference of emotion to object which we should expect from Marvell. But in the latter part of the poem Morris divaricates widely:—

> Yet tottering as I am, and weak,
> Still have I left a little breath
> To seek within the jaws of death
> An entrance to that happy place;
> To seek the unforgotten face
> Once seen, once kissed, once reft from me
> Anigh the murmuring of the sea.

Here the resemblance, if there is any, is to the latter part of "The Coy Mistress." As for the difference, it could not be more pronounced. The effect of Morris's charming poem depends upon the mistiness of the feeling and the vagueness of its object; the effect of Marvell's upon its bright, hard precision. And this precision is not due to the fact that Marvell is concerned with cruder or simpler or more carnal emotions. The emotion of Morris is not more refined or more spiritual; it is merely more vague: if anyone doubts whether the more refined or spiritual emotion can be precise, he should study the treatment of the varieties of discarnate emotion in the

"Paradiso." A curious result of the comparison of Morris's poem with Marvell's is that the former, though it appears to be more serious, is found to be the slighter; and Marvell's "Nymph and Fawn," appearing more slight, is the more serious.

> So weeps the wounded balsam; so
> The holy frankincense doth flow;
> The brotherless Heliades
> Melt in such amber tears as these.

Those verses have the suggestiveness of true poetry; and the verses of Morris, which are nothing if not an attempt to suggest, really suggest nothing; and we are inclined to infer that the suggestiveness is the aura around a bright clear centre, that you cannot have the aura alone. The day-dreamy feeling of Morris is essentially a slight thing; Marvell takes a slight affair, the feeling of a girl for her pet, and gives it a connexion with that inexhaustible and terrible nebula of emotion which surrounds all our exact and practical passions and mingles with them. Again, Marvell does this in a poem which, because of its formal pastoral machinery, may appear a trifling object:—

> *Clorinda:*   Near this, a fountain's liquid bell
>   Tinkles within the concave shell.
> *Damon:*   Might a soul bathe there and be clean,
>   Or slake its drought?

where we find that a metaphor has suddenly rapt us to the image of spiritual purgation. There is here the element of *surprise*, as when Villon says:—

> Necessité faict gens mesprendre
> Et faim saillir le loup des boys,

the surprise which Poe considered of the highest importance, and also the restraint and quietness of tone which make the surprise possible. And in the verses of Marvell which have been quoted there is the making the familiar strange, and the strange familiar, which Coleridge attributed to good poetry.

The effort to construct a dream-world, which alters English poetry so greatly in the nineteenth century, a dream-world utterly different from the visionary realities of the Vita Nuova or of the poetry of Dante's contemporaries, is a problem of which various explanations may no doubt be found; in any case, the result makes a poet of the nineteenth century, of the same size as Marvell, a more trivial and less serious figure. Marvell is no greater personality than William Morris, but he had something much more solid behind him: he had the vast and penetrating influence of Ben Jonson. Jonson never wrote anything so pure as Marvell's Horatian Ode; but this ode has that same quality of wit which was diffused over the whole Elizabethan product and concentrated in the work of Jonson. And, as was said before, this wit which pervades the poetry of Marvell is more Latin, more refined, than anything that succeeded it. The great danger, as well as the great interest and excitement, of English prose and verse, compared with French, is that it permits and justifies an exaggeration of particular qualities to the exclusion of others. Dryden was great in wit, as Milton in magniloquence; but the former, by isolating this quality and making it by itself into great poetry, and the latter, by coming to dispense with it altogether, may perhaps have injured the language. In Dryden wit becomes almost fun, and thereby loses some contact with reality; becomes pure fun, which French wit almost never is.

> The midwife placed her hand on his thick skull,
> With this prophetic blessing: *Be thou dull.*

> A numerous host of dreaming saints succeed,
> Of the true old enthusiastic breed.

This is audacious and splendid; it belongs to satire besides which Marvell's Satires are random babbling; but it is perhaps as exaggerated as—

> Oft he seems to hide his face,
> But unexpectedly returns,
> And to his faithful champion hath in place
> Bore witness gloriously; whence Gaza mourns,
> And all that band them to resist
> His uncontrollable intent.

How oddly the sharp Dantesque phrase "whence Gaza mourns" springs out from the brilliant but ridiculous contortions of Milton's sentence!

> Who from his private gardens, where
> He lived reservèd and austere,
> (As if his highest plot
>   To plant the bergamot)
>
> Could by industrious valour climb
> To ruin the great work of Time,
> And cast the kingdoms old
>   Into another mold;
>
> .   .   .
>
> The Pict no shelter now shall find
> Within his parti-coloured mind,
> But, from this valour sad,
>   Shrink underneath the plaid:

There is an equipoise, a balance and proportion of tones, which, while it cannot raise Marvell to the level of Dryden or Milton, extorts an approval which these poets do not receive from us, and bestows a pleasure at least different in kind from any they can often give. It is what makes Marvell, in the best sense, a classic: classic in a sense in which Gray and Collins are not; for the latter, with all their accredited purity, are comparatively poor in shades of feeling to contrast and unite.

We are baffled in the attempt to translate the quality indicated by the dim and antiquated term wit into the equally unsatisfactory nomenclature of our own time. Even Cowley is only able to define it by negatives:—

> Comely in thousand shapes appears;
>   Yonder we saw it plain; and here 'tis now,
>   Like spirits in a place, we know not how.

It has passed out of our critical coinage altogether, and no new term has been struck to replace it; the quality seldom exists, and is never recognized.

> In a true piece of Wit all things must be
>   Yet all things there agree;
> As in the Ark, join'd without force or strife,
> All creatures dwelt, all creatures that had life.
>   Or as the primitive forms of all
>   (If we compare great things with small)
> Which, without discord or confusion, lie
> In that strange mirror of the Deity.

So far Cowley has spoken well. But if we are to attempt even no more than Cowley, we, placed in a retrospective attitude, must risk much more anxious generalizations. With our eye still on Marvell, we can say that wit is not erudition; it is sometimes stifled by erudition, as in much of Milton. It is not cynicism, though it has a kind of toughness which may be confused with cynicism by the tender-minded. It is confused with erudition because it belongs to an educated mind, rich in generations of experience; and it is confused with cynicism because it implies a constant inspection and criticism of experience. It involves, probably, a recognition, implicit in the expression of every experience, of other kinds of experience which are possible, which we find as clearly in the greatest as in poets like Marvell. Such a general statement may seem to take us a long way from "The Nymph and the Fawn," or even from the Horatian Ode; but it is perhaps justified by the desire to account for that precise taste of Marvell's which finds for him the proper degree of seriousness for every subject which he treats. His errors of taste, when he trespasses, are not sins against this virtue; they are conceits, distended metaphors and similes, but they never consist in taking a subject too seriously or too lightly. This virtue of wit is not a peculiar quality of minor poets, or of the minor poets of one age or of one school; it is an intellectual quality which perhaps only becomes noticeable by itself, in the work of lesser poets. Furthermore, it is absent from the work of Wordsworth, Shelley, and Keats, on whose poetry nineteenth-century criticism has unconsciously been based. To the best of their poetry wit is irrelevant:—

> Art thou pale for weariness
> Of climbing heaven and gazing on the earth,
> Wandering companionless
> Among the stars that have a different birth,
> And ever changing, like a joyless eye,
> That finds no object worth its constancy?

We should find it difficult to draw any useful comparison between these lines of Shelley and anything by Marvell. But later poets, who would have been the better for Marvell's quality, were without it; even Browning seems oddly immature, in some way, beside Marvell. And nowadays we find occasionally good irony, or satire, which lack wit's internal equilibrium, because their voices are essentially protests against some outside sentimentality or stupidity; or we find serious poets who are afraid of acquiring wit, lest they lose intensity. The quality which Marvell had, this modest and certainly impersonal

virtue—whether we call it wit or reason, or even urbanity—
we have patently failed to define. By whatever name we call it,
and however we define that name, it is something precious and
needed and apparently extinct; it is what should preserve the
reputation of Marvel. *C'était une belle âme, comme on ne fait plus à
Londres.*

John Dryden

If the prospect of delight be wanting (which alone justifies the perusal of poetry) we may let the reputation of Dryden sleep in the manuals of literature. To those who are genuinely insensible of his genius (and these are probably the majority of living readers of poetry) we can only oppose illustrations of the following proposition: that their insensibility does not merely signify indifference to satire and wit, but lack of perception of qualities not confined to satire and wit and present in the work of other poets whom these persons feel that they understand. To those whose taste in poetry is formed entirely upon the English poetry of the nineteenth century—to the majority—it is difficult to explain or excuse Dryden: the twentieth century is still the nineteenth, although it may in time acquire its own character. The nineteenth century had, like every other, limited tastes and peculiar fashions; and, like every other, it was unaware of its own limitations. Its tastes and fashions had no place for Dryden; yet Dryden is one of the tests of a catholic appreciation of poetry.

He is a successor of Jonson, and therefore the descendant of Marlowe; he is the ancestor of nearly all that is best in the poetry of the eighteenth century. Once we have mastered Dryden—and by mastery is meant a full and essential enjoyment, not the enjoyment of a private whimsical fashion—we can extract whatever enjoyment and edification there is in his contemporaries—Oldham, Denham, or the less remunerative Waller; and still more his successors—not only Pope, but Phillips, Churchill, Gray, Johnson, Cowper, Goldsmith. His inspiration is prolonged in Crabbe and Byron; it even extends, as Mr. van Doren cleverly points out, to Poe. Even the poets responsible for the revolt were well acquainted with him: Wordsworth knew his work, and Keats invoked his aid. We cannot fully enjoy or rightly estimate a hundred years of English poetry unless we fully enjoy Dryden; and to enjoy Dryden means to pass beyond the limitations of the nineteenth century into a new freedom.

> All, all of a piece throughout:
> Thy Chase had a Beast in View;
> Thy Wars brought nothing about;
> Thy Lovers were all untrue.
> 'Tis well an Old Age is out,
> And time to begin a New.

> . . .

> The world's great age begins anew,
> The golden years return,
> The earth doth like a snake renew
> Her winter weeds outworn:
> Heaven smiles, and faiths and empires gleam
> Like wrecks of a dissolving dream.

The first of these passages is by Dryden, the second by Shelley; the second is found in the "Oxford Book of English Verse," the first is not; yet we might defy anyone to show that the second is superior on intrinsically poetic merit. It is easy to see why the second should appeal more readily to the nineteenth, and what is left of the nineteenth under the name of the twentieth, century. It is not so easy to see propriety in an image which divests a snake of "winter weeds"; and this is a sort of blemish which would have been noticed more quickly by a contemporary of Dryden than by a contemporary of Shelley.

These reflections are occasioned by an admirable book on

Dryden which has appeared at this very turn of time, when taste is becoming perhaps more fluid and ready for a new mould.[1] It is a book which every practitioner of English verse should study. The consideration is so thorough, the matter so compact, the appreciation so just, temperate and enthusiastic, and supplied with such copious and well-chosen extracts from the poetry, the suggestion of astutely placed facts leads our thought so far, that there only remain to mention, as defects which do not detract from its value, two omissions: the prose is not dealt with, and the plays are somewhat slighted. What is especially impressive is the exhibition of the very wide range of Dryden's work, shown by the quotations of every species. Everyone knows "MacFlecknoe," and parts of "Absalom and Achitophel"; in consequence, Dryden has sunk by the persons he has elevated to distinction—Shadwell and Settle, Shaftesbury and Buckingham. Dryden was much more than a satirist; to dispose of him as a satirist is to place an obstacle in the way of our understanding. At all events, we must satisfy ourselves of our definition of the term satire; we must not allow our familiarity with the word to blind us to differences and refinements; we must not assume that satire is a fixed type, and fixed to the prosaic, suited only to prose; we must acknowledge that satire is not the same thing in the hands of two different writers of genius. The connotations of "satire" and of "wit," in short, may be only prejudices of nineteenth-century taste. Perhaps, we think, after reading Mr. van Doren's book, a juster view of Dryden may be given by beginning with some other portion of his work than his celebrated satires; but even here there is much more present, and much more that is poetry, than is usually supposed.

The piece of Dryden's which is the most fun, which is the most sustained display of surprise after surprise of wit from line to line, is "MacFlecknoe." Dryden's method here is something very near to parody; he applies vocabulary, images, and

[1] *John Dryden,* by Mark van Doren (New York: Harcourt, Brace & Howe).

ceremony which arouse epic associations of grandeur, to make an enemy helplessly ridiculous. But the effect, though disastrous for the enemy, is very different from that of the humour which merely belittles, such as the satire of Mark Twain. Dryden continually enhances: he makes his object great, in a way contrary to expectation; and the total effect is due to the transformation of the ridiculous into poetry. As an example may be taken a fine passage plagiarized from Cowley, from lines which Dryden must have marked well, for he quotes them directly in one of his prefaces. Here is Cowley:—

> Where their vast courts the mother-waters keep,
> And undisturbed by moons in silence sleep. . . .
> Beneath the dens where unfledged tempests lie,
> And infant winds their tender voices try.

In "MacFlecknoe" this becomes:—

> Where their vast courts the mother-strumpets keep,
> And undisturbed by watch, in silence sleep.
> Near these, a nursery erects its head,
> Where queens are formed, and future heroes bred;
> Where unfledged actors learn to laugh and cry,
> Where infant punks their tender voices try,
> And little Maximins the gods defy.

The passage from Cowley is by no means despicable verse. But it is a commonplace description of commonly poetic objects; it has not the element of *surprise* so essential to poetry, and this Dryden provides. A clever versifier might have written Cowley's lines; only a poet could have made what Dryden made of them. It is impossible to dismiss his verses as "prosaic"; turn them into prose and they are transmuted, the fragrance is gone. The reproach of the prosaic, levelled at Dryden, rests upon a confusion between the emotions considered to be poetic, which is a matter allowing considerable latitude of fashion, and the result of personal emotion in poetry;

and, in the third place, there is the emotion depicted by the poet in some kinds of poetry, of which the "Testaments" of Villon is an example. Again, there is the intellect, the originality and independence and clarity of what we vaguely call the poet's "point of view." Our valuation of poetry, in short, depends upon several considerations, upon the permanent and upon the mutable and upon the transitory. When we try to isolate the essentially poetic, we bring our pursuit in the end to something insignificant; our standards vary with every poet whom we consider. All we can hope to do, in the attempt to introduce some order into our preferences, is to clarify our reasons for finding pleasure in the poetry that we like.

With regard to Dryden, therefore, we can say this much. Our taste in English poetry has been largely founded upon a partial perception of the value of Shakespeare and Milton, a perception which dwells upon sublimity of theme and action. Shakespeare had a great deal more; he had nearly everything to satisfy our various desires for poetry. The point is that the depreciation or neglect of Dryden is not due to the fact that his work is not poetry, but to a prejudice that the material, the feelings, out of which he built it is not poetic. Thus Matthew Arnold observes, in mentioning Dryden and Pope together, that "their poetry is conceived and composed in their wits, genuine poetry is conceived in the soul." Arnold was, perhaps, not altogether the detached critic when he wrote this line; he may have been stirred to a defence of his own poetry, conceived and composed in the soul of a mid-century Oxford graduate. Pater remarks that Dryden—

> Loved to emphasize the distinction between poetry and prose, the protest against their confusion coming with somewhat diminished effect from one whose poetry was so prosaic.

But Dryden was right, and the sentence of Pater is cheap journalism. Hazlitt, who had perhaps the most uninteresting mind of all our distinguished critics, says:—

Dryden and Pope are the great masters of the artificial style of poetry in our language, as the poets of whom I have already treated—Chaucer, Spenser, Shakespeare, and Milton—were of the natural.

In one sentence Hazlitt has committed at least four crimes against taste. It is bad enough to lump Chaucer, Spenser, Shakespeare, and Milton together under the denomination of "natural"; it is bad to commit Shakespeare to one style only; it is bad to join Dryden and Pope together; but the last absurdity is the contrast of Milton, our greatest master of the *artificial* style, with Dryden, whose *style* (vocabulary, syntax, and order of thought) is in a high degree natural. And what all these objections come to, we repeat, is a repugnance for the material out of which Dryden's poetry is built.

It would be truer to say, indeed, even in the form of the unpersuasive paradox, that Dryden is distinguished principally by his *poetic* ability. We prize him, as we do Mallarmé, for what he made of his material. Our estimate is only in part the appreciation of ingenuity: in the end the result *is* poetry. Much of Dryden's unique merit consists in his ability to make the small into the great, the prosaic into the poetic, the trivial into the magnificent. In this he differs not only from Milton, who required a canvas of the largest size, but from Pope, who required one of the smallest. If you compare any satiric "character" of Pope with one of Dryden, you will see that the method and intention are widely divergent. When Pope alters, he diminishes; he is a master of miniature. The singular skill of his portrait of Addison, for example, in the "Epistle to Arbuthnot," depends upon the justice and reserve, the apparent determination not to exaggerate. The genius of Pope is not for caricature. But the effect of the portraits of Dryden is to transform the object into something greater, as were transformed the verses of Cowley quoted above.

> A fiery soul, which working out its way,
> Fretted the pigmy body to decay:
> And o'er informed the tenement of clay.

These lines are not merely a magnificent tribute. They create the object which they contemplate; the poetry is purer than anything in Pope except the last lines of the "Dunciad." Dryden is in fact much nearer to the master of comic creation than to Pope. As in Jonson, the effect is far from laughter; the comic is the material, the result is poetry. The Civic Guards of Rhodes—

> The country rings around with loud alarms,
> And raw in fields the rude militia swarms;
> Mouths without hands; maintained at vast expense,
> In peace a charge, in war a weak defence;
> Stout once a month they march, a blust'ring band,
> And ever, but in times of need, at hand;
> This was the morn, when issuing on the guard,
> Drawn up in rank and file they stood prepared
> Of seeming arms to make a short essay,
> Then hasten to be drunk, the business of the day.

Sometimes the wit appears as a delicate flavour to the magnificence, as in "Alexander's Feast":—

> Sooth'd with the sound the king grew vain;
> Fought all his battles o'er again;
> And thrice he routed all his foes, and thrice
>   he slew the slain.

The great advantage of Dryden over Milton is that while the former is always in control of his ascent, and can rise or fall at will (and how masterfully, like his own Timotheus, he directs the transitions!), the latter has elected a perch from which he cannot afford to fall, and from which he is in danger of slipping.

food alike those pure
Intelligential substances require
As doth your Rational; and both contain
Within them every lower faculty
Of sense, whereby they hear, see, smell, touch, taste,
Tasting concoct, digest, assimilate,
And corporeal to incorporeal turn.

Dryden might have made poetry out of that; his translation from Lucretius is poetry. But we have an ingenious example, on which to test our contrast of Dryden and Milton: it is Dryden's "Opera," called *The State of Innocence and Fall of Man*, of which Nathaniel Lee neatly says in his preface:—

For Milton did the wealthy mine disclose,
And rudely cast what you could well dispose:
He roughly drew, on an old-fashioned ground,
A chaos, for no perfect world were found,
Till through the heap, your mighty genius shined.

In the author's preface Dryden acknowledges his debt generously enough:—

The original being undoubtedly, one of the greatest, most noble, and most sublime poems, which either this age or nation has produced.

The poem begins auspiciously:—

Lucifer: Is this the seat our conqueror has given?
And this the climate we must change for Heaven?
These regions and this realm my wars have got;
This mournful empire is the loser's lot:
In liquid burnings, or on dry to dwell,
Is all the sad variety of Hell.

It is an early work; it is on the whole a feeble work; it is not deserving of sustained comparison with "Paradise Lost." But "all the sad variety of Hell"! Dryden is already stirring; he has assimilated what he could from Milton; and he has shown himself capable of producing as splendid verse.

The capacity for assimilation, and the consequent extent of range, are conspicuous qualities of Dryden. He advanced and exhibited his variety by constant translation; and his translations of Horace, of Ovid, of Lucretius, are admirable. His gravest defects are supposed to be displayed in his dramas, but if these were more read they might be more praised. From the point of view of either the Elizabethan or the French drama they are obviously inferior; but the charge of inferiority loses part of its force if we admit that Dryden was not quite trying to compete with either, but was pursuing a direction of his own. He created no character; and although his arrangements of plot manifest exceptional ingenuity, it is the pure magnificence of diction, of poetic diction, that keeps his plays alive:—

> How I loved
> Witness ye days and nights, and all ye hours,
> That danced away with down upon your feet,
> As all your business were to count my passion.
> One day passed by, and nothing saw but love;
> Another came, and still 'twas only love:
> The suns were wearied out with looking on,
> And I untired with loving.
> I saw you every day and all the day;
> And every day was still but as the first:
> So eager was I still to see you more ...
>
> While within your arms I lay,
> The world fell mould'ring from my hands each hour.

Such language is pure Dryden: it sounds, in Mr. van Doren's phrase, "like a gong." *All for Love*, from which the lines are taken, is Dryden's best play, and this is perhaps the highest reach. In general, he is best in his plays when dealing with situations which do not demand great emotional concentration; when his situation is more trivial, and he can practise his art of making the small great. The back-talk between the Emperor and his Empress Nourmahal, in *Aurungzebe*, is admirable purple comedy:—

Emperor: Such virtue is the plague of human life:
             A virtuous woman, but a cursèd wife.
             In vain of pompous chastity y' are proud:
             Virtue's adultery of the tongue, when loud.
             I, with less pain, a prostitute could bear,
             Than the shrill sound of virtue, virtue hear.
             In unchaste wives—
             There's yet a kind of recompensing ease:
             Vice keeps 'em humble, gives 'em care to please:
             But against clamourous virtue, what defence?
             It stops our mouths, and gives your noise pretence. . . .

             What can be sweeter than our native home?
             Thither for ease, and soft repose, we come;
             Home is the sacred refuse of our life:
             Secure from all approaches but a wife.
             If thence we fly, the cause admits no doubt:
             None but an inmate foe could force us out.
             Clamours, our privacies uneasy make:
             Birds leave their nests disturbed, and
                 beasts their haunts forsake.

But drama is a mixed form; pure magnificence will not carry it through. The poet who attempts to achieve a play by the single force of the word provokes comparison, however strictly he confine himself to his capacity, with poets of other gifts. Corneille and Racine do not attain their triumphs by magnificence of this sort; they have concentration also, and, in the midst of their phrases, an undisturbed attention to the human soul as they knew it.

Nor is Dryden unchallenged in his supreme ability to make the ridiculous, or the trivial, great.

> Avez-vous observé que maints cercueils de vielles
> Sont presque aussi petits que celui d'un enfant?

Those lines are the work of a man whose verse is as magnificent as Dryden's, and who could see profounder possibilities in wit, and in Dryden's mind. For Dryden, with all his intellect, had a commonplace mind. His powers were, we believe, wider, but no greater, than Milton's; he was confined by boundaries as impassable, though less strait. He bears a curious antithetical resemblance to Swinburne. Swinburne was also a master of words, but Swinburne's words are all suggestions and no detonation; if they suggest nothing, it is because they suggest too much. Dryden's words, on the other hand, are precise, they state immensely, but their suggestiveness is almost nothing.

> That short dark passage to a future state;
> That melancholy riddle of a breath.
> That something, or that nothing, after death,

is a riddle, but not melancholy enough, in Dryden's splendid verse. The question, which has certainly been waiting, may justly be asked: whether without this which Dryden lacks, poetry can exist? What is man to decide what poetry is? Dryden's use of language is not, like that of Swinburne, weakening and demoralizing. Let us take as a final test his elegy upon Oldham, which deserves not to be mutilated:—

> Farewell, too little and too lately known,
> Whom I began to think and call my own;
> For sure our souls were near allied, and thine
> Cast in the same poetic mould with mine.
> One common note on either lyre did strike,
> And knaves and fools we both abhorred alike.
> To the same goal did both our studies drive;
> The last set out the soonest did arrive.
> Thus Nisus fell upon the slippery place,

Whilst his young friend performed and won the race.
O early ripe! to thy abundant store
What could advancing age have added more?
It might (what nature never gives the young)
Have taught the numbers of thy native tongue.
But satire needs not those, and wit will shine
Through the harsh cadence of a rugged line.
A noble error, and but seldom made,
When poets are by too much force betrayed.
Thy generous fruits, though gathered ere their prime,
Still showed a quickness; and maturing time
But mellows what we write to the dull sweets of rhyme.
Once more, hail, and farewell; farewell, thou young,
But ah! too short, Marcellus of our tongue!
Thy brows with ivy and with laurels bound;
But fate and gloomy night encompass thee around.

From the perfection of such an elegy we cannot detract; the
lack of nebula is compensated by the satisfying completeness
of the statement. Dryden lacked what his master Jonson pos-
sessed, a large and unique view of life; he lacked insight, he
lacked profundity. But where Dryden fails to satisfy, the nine-
teenth century does not satisfy us either; and where that cen-
tury has condemned him, it is itself condemned. In the next
revolution of taste it is possible that poets may turn to the
study of Dryden. He remains one of those who have set stan-
dards for English verse which it is desperate to ignore.

THE METAPHYSICAL POETS

By collecting these poems[1] from the work of a generation more often named than read, and more often read than profitably studied, Professor Grierson has rendered a service of some importance. Certainly the reader will meet with many poems already preserved in other anthologies, at the same time that he discovers poems such as those of Aurelian Townshend or Lord Herbert of Cherbury here included. But the function of such an anthology as this is neither that of Professor Saintsbury's admirable edition of Caroline poets nor that of the "Oxford Book of English Verse." Mr. Grierson's book is in itself a piece of criticism, and a provocation of criticism; and we think that he was right in including so many poems of Donne, elsewhere (though not in many editions) accessible, as documents in the case of "metaphysical poetry." The phrase has long done duty as a term of abuse, or as the label of a quaint and pleasant taste. The question is to what extent the so-called metaphysicals formed a school (in our own time we should say a "movement"), and how far this so-called school or movement is a digression from the main current.

[1] *Metaphysical Lyrics and Poems of the Seventeenth Century: Donne to Butler.* Selected and edited, with an Essay, by Herbert J. C. Grierson (Oxford: Clarendon Press. London: Milford).

Not only is it extremely difficult to define metaphysical poetry, but difficult to decide what poets practise it and in which of their verses. The poetry of Donne (to whom Marvell and Bishop King are sometimes nearer than any of the other authors) is late Elizabethan, its feeling often very close to that of Chapman. The "courtly" poetry is derivative from Jonson, who borrowed liberally from the Latin; it expires in the next century with the sentiment and witticism of Prior. There is finally the devotional verse of Herbert, Vaughan and Crashaw (echoed long after by Christina Rossetti and Francis Thompson); Crashaw, sometimes more profound and less sectarian than the others, has a quality which returns through the Elizabethan period to the early Italians. It is difficult to find any precise use of metaphor, simile, or other conceit, which is common to all the poets and at the same time important enough as an element of style to isolate these poets as a group. Donne, and often Cowley, employ a device which is sometimes considered characteristically "metaphysical": the elaboration (contrasted with the condensation) of a figure of speech to the farthest stage to which ingenuity can carry it. Thus Cowley develops the commonplace comparison of the world to a chess-board through long stanzas ("To Destiny"), and Donne, with more grace, in "A Valediction," the comparison of two lovers to a pair of compasses. But elsewhere we find, instead of the mere explication of the content of a comparison, a development by rapid association of thought which requires considerable agility on the part of the reader.

> On a round ball
> A workeman that hath copies by, can lay
> An Europe, Afrique, and an Asia.
> And quickly make that, which was nothing, *All*,
>   So doth each teare,
>   Which thee doth weare,
> A globe, yea world by that impression grow,
> Till thy tears mixt with mine doe overflow

> This world, by waters sent from thee, my
> heaven dissolved so.

Here we find at least two connexions which are not implicit in the first figure, but are forced upon it by the poet: from the geographer's globe to the tear, and the tear to the deluge. On the other hand, some of Donne's most successful and characteristic effects are secured by brief words and sudden contrasts:—

> A bracelet of bright hair about the bone,

where the most powerful effect is produced by the sudden contrast of associations of "bright hair" and of "bone." This telescoping of images and multiplied association is characteristic of the phrase of some of the dramatists of the period which Donne knew: not to mention Shakespeare, it is frequent in Middleton, Webster and Tourneur, and is one of the sources of the vitality of their language.

Johnson, who employed the term "metaphysical poets," apparently having Donne, Cleveland and Cowley chiefly in mind, remarks of them that "the most heterogenous ideas are yoked by violence together." The force of this impeachment lies in the failure of the conjunction, the fact that often the ideas are yoked but not united; and if we are to judge of styles of poetry by their abuse, enough examples may be found in Cleveland to justify Johnson's condemnation. But a degree of heterogeneity of material compelled into unity by the operation of the poet's mind is omnipresent in poetry. We need not select for illustration such a line as:—

> Notre âme est un trois-mâts cherchant son Icarie;

we may find it in some of the best lines of Johnson himself ("The Vanity of Human Wishes"):—

His fate was destined to a barren strand,
A petty fortress, and a dubious hand;
He left a name at which the world grew pale,
To point a moral, or adorn a tale,

where the effect is due to a contrast of ideas, different in degree but the same principle, as that which Johnson mildly reprehended. And in one of the finest poems of the age (a poem which could not have been written in any other age), the "Exequy" of Bishop King, the extended comparison is used with perfect success: the idea and the simile become one, in the passage in which the Bishop illustrates his impatience to see his dead wife, under the figure of a journey:—

Stay for me there; I will not faile
To meet thee in that hollow Vale.
And think not much of my delay;
I am already on the way,
And follow thee with all the speed
Desire can make, or sorrows breed.
Each minute is a short degree.
And ev'ry houre a step towards thee.
At night when I betake to rest,
Next morn I rise nearer my West
Of life, almost by eight houres sail,
Than when sleep breath'd his drowsy gale. . . .
But heark! My Pulse, like a soft Drum
Beats my approach, tells *Thee* I come;
And slow howere my marches be,
I shall at last sit down by *Thee.*

(In the last few lines there is that effect of terror which is several times attained by one of Bishop King's admirers, Edgar Poe). Again, we may justly take these quatrains from Lord Herbert's Ode, stanzas which would, we think, be immediately pronounced to be of the metaphysical school:—

So when from hence we shall be gone,
        And be no more, nor you, nor I,
        As one another's mystery,
Each shall be both, yet both but one.

This said, in her up-lifted face,
        Her eyes, which did that beauty crown,
        Were like two starrs, that having faln down,
Look up again to find their place:

While such a moveless silent peace
        Did seize on their becalmed sense,
        One would have thought some influence
Their ravished spirits did possess.

There is nothing in these lines (with the possible exception of the stars, a simile not at once grasped, but lovely and justified) which fits Johnson's general observations on the metaphysical poets in his essay on Cowley. A good deal resides in the richness of association which is at the same time borrowed from and given to the word "becalmed"; but the meaning is clear, the language simple and elegant. It is to be observed that the language of these poets is as a rule simple and pure; in the verse of George Herbert this simplicity is carried as far as it can go—a simplicity emulated without success by numerous modern poets. The *structure* of the sentences, on the other hand, is sometimes far from simple, but this is not a vice: it is a fidelity to thought and feeling. The effect, at its best, is far less artificial than that of an ode by Gray. And as this fidelity induces variety of thought and feeling, so it induces variety of music. We doubt whether, in the eighteenth century, could be found two poems in nominally the same metre, so dissimilar as Marvell's "Coy Mistress" and Crashaw's "Saint Teresa"; the one producing an effect of great speed by the use of short syllables, and the other an ecclesiastical solemnity by the use of long ones:—

> Love, thou art absolute sole lord
> Of life and death.

If so shrewd and sensitive (though so limited) a critic as Johnson failed to define metaphysical poetry by its faults, it is worth while to inquire whether we may not have more success by adopting the opposite method: by assuming that the poets of the seventeenth century (up to the Revolution) were the direct and normal development of the precedent age; and, without prejudicing their case by the adjective "metaphysical," consider whether their virtue was not something permanently valuable, which subsequently disappeared, but ought not to have disappeared. Johnson has hit, perhaps by accident, on one of their peculiarities when he observes that "their attempts were always analytic"; he would not agree that, after the dissociation, they put the material together again in a new unity.

It is certain that the dramatic verse of the later Elizabethan and early Jacobean poets expresses a degree of development of sensibility which is not found in any of the prose, good as it often is. If we except Marlowe, a man of prodigious intelligence, these dramatists were directly or indirectly (it is at least a tenable theory) affected by Montaigne. Even if we except also Jonson and Chapman, these two were notably erudite, and were notably men who incorporated their erudition into their sensibility: their mode of feeling was directly and freshly altered by their reading and thought. In Chapman especially there is a direct sensuous apprehension of thought into feeling, which is exactly what we find in Donne:—

> in this one thing, all the discipline
> Of manners and of manhood is contained;
> A man to join himself with th' Universe
> In his main sway, and make in all things fit
> One with that All, and go on, round as it;
> Not plucking from the whole his wretched part,

And into straits, or into nought revert,
Wishing the complete Universe might be
Subject to such a rag of it as he;
But to consider great Necessity.

We compare this with some modern passage:—

No, when the fight begins within himself,
A man's worth something. God stoops o'er his head,
Satan looks up between his feet—both tug—
He's left, himself, i' the middle; the soul wakes
And grows. Prolong that battle through his life!

It is perhaps somewhat less fair, though very tempting (as both poets are concerned with the perpetuation of love by offspring), to compare with the stanzas already quoted from Lord Herbert's Ode the following from Tennyson:—

One walked between his wife and child,
With measured footfall firm and mild,
And now and then he gravely smiled.
   The prudent partner of his blood
   Leaned on him, faithful, gentle, good,
   Wearing the rose of womanhood.
And in their double love secure,
The little maiden walked demure,
Pacing with downward eyelids pure.
   These three made unity so sweet,
   My frozen heart began to beat,
   Remembering its ancient heat.

The difference is not a simple difference of degree between poets. It is something which had happened to the mind of England between the time of Donne or Lord Herbert of Cherbury and the time of Tennyson and Browning; it is the difference between the intellectual poet and the reflective poet. Tennyson and Browning are poets, and they think; but they do not feel their thought as immediately as the odour of a rose. A thought to Donne was an experience; it modified his sensibility. When a poet's mind is perfectly equipped for its work, it is constantly amalgamating disparate experience; the ordinary man's experience is chaotic, irregular, fragmentary. The latter falls in love, or reads Spinoza, and these two experiences have nothing to do with each other, or with the noise of the typewriter or the smell of cooking; in the mind of the poet these experiences are always forming new wholes.

We may express the difference by the following theory: The poets of the seventeenth century, the successors of the dramatists of the sixteenth, possessed a mechanism of sensibility which could devour any kind of experience. They are simple, artificial, difficult, or fantastic, as their predecessors were; no less nor more than Dante, Guido Cavalcanti, Guinizelli, or Cino. In the seventeenth century a dissociation of sensibility set in, from which we have never recovered; and this dissociation, as is natural, was due to the influence of the two most powerful poets of the century, Milton and Dryden. Each of these men performed certain poetic functions so magnificently well that the magnitude of the effect concealed the absence of others. The language went on and in some respects improved; the best verse of Collins, Gray, Johnson, and even Goldsmith satisfies some of our fastidious demands better than that of Donne or Marvell or King. But while the language became more refined, the feeling became more crude. The feeling, the sensibility, expressed in the "Country Churchyard" (to say nothing of Tennyson and Browning) is cruder than that in the "Coy Mistress."

The second effect of the influence of Milton and Dryden followed from the first, and was therefore slow in manifestation. The sentimental age began early in the eighteenth century, and continued. The poets revolted against the ratiocinative, the descriptive; they thought and felt by fits, unbalanced; they reflected. In one or two passages of Shelley's "Triumph of Life," in the second "Hyperion," there are traces of a struggle toward unification of sensibility. But Keats and Shelley died, and Tennyson and Browning ruminated.

After this brief exposition of a theory—too brief, perhaps, to carry conviction—we may ask, what would have been the fate of the "metaphysical" had the current of poetry descended in a direct line from them, as it descended in a direct line to them? They would not, certainly, be classified as metaphysical. The possible interests of a poet are unlimited; the more intelligent he is the better; the more intelligent he is the more likely that he will have interests: our only condition is that he turn them into poetry, and not merely meditate on them poetically. A philosophical theory which has entered into poetry is established, for its truth or falsity in one sense ceases to matter, and its truth in another sense is proved. The poets in question have, like other poets, various faults. But they were, at best, engaged in the task of trying to find the verbal equivalent for states of mind and feeling. And this means both that they are more mature, and that they wear better, than later poets of certainly not less literary ability.

It is not a permanent necessity that poets should be interested in philosophy, or in any other subject. We can only say that it appears likely that poets in our civilization, as it exists at present, must be *difficult*. Our civilization comprehends great variety and complexity, and this variety and complexity, playing upon a refined sensibility, must produce various and complex results. The poet must become more and more comprehensive, more allusive, more indirect, in order to force, to dislocate if necessary, language into his meaning. (A brilliant and extreme statement of this view, with which it is not requisite to associate oneself, is that of M. Jean Epstein, "La Poésie d'aujourd'hui.") Hence we get something which looks very much like the conceit—we get, in fact, a method curiously similar to that of the "metaphysical poets," similar also in its use of obscure words and of simple phrasing.

O géraniums diaphanes, guerroyeurs sortilèges,
Sacrilèges monomanes!
Emballages, dévergondages, douches! O pressoirs
Des vendanges des grands soirs!
Layettes aux abois,
Thyrses au fond des bois!
Transfusions, représailles,
Relevailles, compresses et l'éternal potion,
Angélus! n'en pouvoir plus
De débâcles nuptiales! de débâcles nuptiales!

The same poet could write also simply:—

Elle est bien loin, elle pleure,
Le grand vent se lamente aussi ...

Jules Laforgue, and Tristan Corbière in many of his poems, are nearer to the "school of Donne" than any modern English poet. But poets more classical than they have the same essential quality of transmuting ideas into sensations, of transforming an observation into a state of mind.

Pour l'enfant, amoureux de cartes et d'estampes,
L'univers est égal à son vaste appétit.
Ah, que le monde est grand à la clarté des lampes!
Aux yeux du souvenir que le monde est petit!

In French literature the great master of the seventeenth century—Racine—and the great master of the nineteenth—Baudelaire—are more like each other than they are like anyone else. The greatest two masters of diction are also the greatest two psychologists, the most curious explorers of the soul. It is interesting to speculate whether it is not a misfortune that two of the greatest masters of diction in our language, Milton and Dryden, triumph with a dazzling disregard of the soul. If we continued to produce Miltons and Drydens it might not so much matter, but as things are it is a pity that

English poetry has remained so incomplete. Those who object to the "artificiality" of Milton or Dryden sometimes tell us to "look into our hearts and write." But that is not looking deep enough; Racine or Donne looked into a good deal more than the heart. One must look into the cerebral cortex, the nervous system, and the digestive tracts.

May we not conclude, then, that Donne, Crashaw, Vaughan, Herbert and Lord Herbert, Marvell, King, Cowley at his best, are in the direct current of English poetry, and that their faults should be reprimanded by this standard rather than coddled by antiquarian affection? They have been enough praised in terms which are implicit limitations because they are "metaphysical" or "witty," "quaint" or "obscure," though at their best they have not these attributes more than other serious poets. On the other hand, we must not reject the criticism of Johnson (a dangerous person to disagree with) without having mastered it, without having assimilated the Johnsonian canons of taste. In reading the celebrated passage in his essay on Cowley we must remember that by wit he clearly means something more serious than we usually mean to-day; in his criticism of their versification we must remember in what a narrow discipline he was trained, but also how well trained; we must remember that Johnson tortures chiefly the chief offenders, Cowley and Cleveland. It would be a fruitful work, and one requiring a substantial book, to break up the classification of Johnson (for there has been none since) and exhibit these poets in all their difference of kind and of degree, from the massive music of Donne to the faint, pleasing tinkle of Aurelian Townshend—whose "Dialogue between a Pilgrim and Time" is one of the few regrettable omissions from this excellent anthology.

A NOTE ON THE TYPE

The principal text of this Modern Library edition
was set in a digitized version of Janson,
a typeface that dates from about 1690 and was cut by Nicholas Kis,
a Hungarian working in Amsterdam. The original matrices have
survived and are held by the Stempel foundry in Germany.
Hermann Zapf redesigned some of the weights and sizes for Stempel,
basing his revisions on the original design.